WALKING BACK TO ME

WALKING
BACK
TO ME

THE RAMBLINGS OF A
WANDERING WIDOW

CLAIRE RUSSELL

ISBN 9781916206007

Published by Sansevieria
Anerley
London
SE20 7RW

Edited by Sophie Lazar
Typeset by seagulls.net
Cover design by Lesley Gilmour

For Jimmy and all his love

* * * * * * * * * * *

'How many loved your moments of glad grace,
And loved your beauty with love false or true,
But one man loved the pilgrim soul in you,
And loved the sorrows of your changing face…'

William Butler Yeats

PROLOGUE

MY SLIDING-DOORS LIFE

Have I told you yet that I'm a widow? No? Don't worry I soon will, I tell everyone. I'm like the old person at the bus stop who tells you their age. It's a compulsion I've developed and I can't maintain a conversation with you unless you know; it just feels wrong. I'm different, you see, not like you. I might look fairly normal but I'm really not. I understand now why widows used to wear a distinct uniform – marking them out. You'd see a woman dressed head to toe in 'Widow's Weeds' and instantly know the deal but I can't do that so I have to tell you or I feel somehow disingenuous, like I'm misleading you. Or perhaps the truth is that the more I say it out loud, the closer I'll be to accepting this unimaginable situation.

But let us rewind. It's 14 December. At 6.30am I'm nagging my husband, Jimmy, for snoring. By 8.30am I'm standing in Lewisham A&E taking the wedding ring off of his dead hand and being given a booklet entitled 'Bereavement'. Merry Christmas, God bless us every one.

And just like that I've a new moniker – widow. Instantly I'm exiled to a strange foreign country. What I had believed to be a lifetime visa to happiness has been revoked and it seems as if I will never get my passport back to normality. From the moment I got together with Jimmy five years earlier, I knew it was all going to be just fine. I never had any doubt about whether he was 'the one'. I felt whole, complete. He wasn't so much the 'wind beneath my wings' but he held the kite string so I could fly freely. And now he was gone, soon to be reduced to ashes in an urn in a bag in my dressing room. Who am I now? I keep looking but I just can't find myself and it's terrifying.

Life soon becomes a matter of existence and a dreadful fear sets in. The landscape that was my life with Jimmy has been ripped away with just a huge void of pain ahead of me. No one can help, nothing can help. I don't want anything, I can't see the point to anything. Loneliness is such an inadequate word for it. Jimmy was everything to me and me to him. We were together constantly and had our life mapped out, and it was a good one, it really was.

In my sliding-doors life we would have had Jimmy's family over for Christmas for the first time, a clan gathering (he was Scottish). We'd ordered the turkey and the crackers and were rushing to get the house renovations finished in time. Jimmy had wanted to put the Christmas tree up early he was so excited and I insisted we wait until I'd finished work, which would have been 16 December. But instead of the anticipated festivities the Christmas cards abruptly stopped and the sympathy cards started flooding in. Now, instead of organising menus I was organising a funeral. Instead of buying gifts I was buying flowers. There was no Christmas tree.

With Jimmy I'd felt charmed, I'd felt different. I had found the love of my life and hadn't 'settled'. I'd waited and my patience had paid off with dividends. I had a brilliant, handsome, gentle soul as my husband and so by association surely that must mean I was an okay person after all. He had chosen me and being loved by such a beautiful man gave me self-respect, dignity and safety for the first time in my life. I was almost 40 at the time and Jimmy was heading for 50, having never been married before (although he had a lovely son). His reputation preceded him as being a BAFTA-winning screenwriter and he was spoken of in the TV industry in hallowed terms. When I got the job of working with him I was quite apprehensive at first. However, I soon found that he was a typical writer: rarely getting his scripts in on time and he was forever disappearing off on trips. I used to imagine him in a stripy red-and-white outfit off travelling and referred to him as 'Where's Jimmy?' But then something shifted. The project we were doing was a book adaptation and it was quite tricky, so we used to talk about anything but the project and in this way got to know and like one another very much. We were definitely good friends before anything else. Funnily enough, my boss and Jimmy's good friend had told me when I started working with him that 'Jimmy doesn't keep good health'.

Jimmy had to have an autopsy as he had died so suddenly, although it was clear that the cause was his heart. He'd been born with a hole in it and had had to manage his health since then. We couldn't have the funeral until 29 December. I threw myself into organisational mode. I organised flowers, I sorted out music; most importantly I chose my outfit. The pink Cromby coat that I wore on our first proper date in Edinburgh several years ago that Jimmy loved so much. I had to get it from the dry cleaners where Jimmy had put it the week before he died. He hated winter but he said the one consolation was seeing me in that coat.

January came and slowly everyone went back to their lives and I looked ahead at the next year bewildered. Nothing, not one thing, was the same. I thought it ironic that I had wanted to lose a few pounds for Christmas and there I was, the thinnest I had been since I was a teenager. The grief diet is a very effective one. There was absolutely no way I could eat, it seemed such a very odd thing to do. To eat you have to have an appetite, you have to 'want' food, and I wanted nothing. Well, perhaps the obliteration a bottle of wine might offer.

At the beginning of a new year I had always enjoyed working out the coming 365 days; looking at a new diary with excitement and happily filling in the blank dates with events. But this year was different; I did buy a diary as there were indeed things that I had to put in it but none of them were things to look forward to, nothing I'd chosen to do. I found myself just flicking through all those blank pages without a clue of how they would pan out.

The grief tourists came and went, they offered pockets of distraction from the landscape of despair. Yes, it was a lovely service, and yes, wasn't I brave to stand up and read the eulogy I'd written. No, I wasn't brave at all – quite the opposite. The thought of walking into my beautiful husband's cremation four days after Christmas was too enormous to get my head around. If I turned it into a performance the nervousness associated with standing up in front of all those folk would override the reality of the situation and I could at least get through the door of the chapel.

A sort of insanity set in, a whole new reality offering itself up as 'normality'. It was perfectly normal to have all the radios turned on in the house but with the sound turned down to zero. It was obviously now normal to spend hours watching re-runs of *Poirot*, *Rosemary and Thyme* and *Midsomer Murders* and then top the day off with *Schindler's List*. Nothing in between. I'm a very black or white person with no grey areas. It was normal to stay in bed till around one o'clock each day – what was the point in getting up?

Around February I figured this was an existence that I wanted no more truck with and hunted round for a bunch of Jimmy's tablets, necked a bottle of wine and took an entire blister pack, putting myself to bed. And bugger me, I woke up. Here's a top tip for would-be suicidal widows who are long-sighted: make sure you have your glasses to hand when taking the pills to at least see what you are taking. I couldn't find mine and it turned out it was fairly harmless stuff I had taken – so now what to do? It seemed somehow rude to try again and I was pretty sure that Dignitas wouldn't consider grief a genuine cause (shame, because I love Switzerland). So I had to look at this life, see if there was any way to carve out something that would some day feel ok, tailor something that would one day fit me. Could time possibly heal as everyone claimed? Was my old friend right to say, 'it's worth sticking around to see how it all turns out in the end'?

CHAPTER 1

CAMINO ROYAL

By the following May, every day was still such a struggle but I was somehow getting through each one. I took in a lodger as I had no means of income and was still struggling to even leave the house let alone go to and function in a proper job. And so Lisa came into my life. A lovely yoga teacher with a great sense of humour as well as a shining spirituality who told me about the ancient pilgrimage grandly named the Camino de Santiago de Compostela. As she described it I found myself actually feeling something: a response, a sense of wanting. Lisa could see my enthusiasm but looked doubtful when I expressed interest in taking part myself, mumbling something about it being very 'basic'. For those of you who don't know me, I should make it clear that I do have an appreciation of the more comfortable elements in life. Jimmy used to say I was the 'princess in exile'. This is true to a degree but I have also been known to rough it quite happily. I'm fine with either extreme, it's mediocrity that I dislike. I pointed out to Lisa that I didn't feel spiritual awakenings and en suite bathrooms needed to be mutually exclusive.

I became obsessed with going on the walk, and doing some research I found a travel company who booked hopefully comfy hotels and baggage transfers along the route, along with hot meals waiting for me at the end of the day. No hair shirts for me. I know Jimmy would have expected nothing less. He loved being married to a princess. He could keep his man-of-the-people image and yet indulge in the luxury he secretly adored, throwing his hands up, and rolling his eyes convincingly in my direction with a 'what's a guy to do?' expression. I was happy to play along; he used to joke that I aspired to be shallow. I had a strong feeling that maybe, just maybe, along this spiritual pilgrimage covering the steps of thousands before me I might begin to find myself again. Maybe I could walk back to me?

I've always loved a huge challenge; Jimmy used to say I was stubborn but, it's that black and white thing. Once I put my mind to something it will happen – it might take a while but it will eventually come to pass. Here's a random example: when I was eleven I was obsessed with going to Disneyland. Completely and utterly obsessed. It was never going to happen at that time, to go to America was beyond my comprehension and my family's pocket, but the desire consumed me. Years later I would not only end up working at the Disney Studios in California but also have my work's Christmas 'do' at the theme park.

Grief is an indiscriminate taker, it gives nothing and takes everything, especially choices and freedom, so I figured a good walk might be just the thing to counter that impotency. And let's face it, when the 'where are you going on holiday this year?' conversation comes up, it's great to just drop into the conversation that you are off to walk across Spain.

So here I am nine months after the worst day of my life, with a package of travel documents, a pair of walking boots and the first fleece I have *ever* owned. Lisa kindly helped me to navigate the 'outdoorsy type' shops in Covent Garden and I even got a pac-a-mac. The countdown's on and I find myself getting increasingly nervous and wondering if I can actually do this. Supposing I can't? What then? The itinerary tells me I fly to Madrid then take a five-hour bus trip to Leon to stay the night in a hotel and start the walk the following morning. It's just over 300 kilometres, which really does seem quite a long way, especially as I've been known to drive my car to the local corner shop, and only twelve days to complete it in.

I've made the decision not to listen to music along the way or take my computer. I want to take the twelve days to indulge in looking at the wonderful years I had with Jimmy and also to explore the vagaries of grief. Grief has become a very loyal companion over these past months, never leaving my side, so I know I have to develop a relationship with it. There's no way you can ignore it so I want to take this time to get better acquainted with it and hopefully change our relationship to something we are both comfortable with.

Until Leon then…

CHAPTER 2

KINGS OF LEON

It's 3 September, the day after my birthday. Jimmy and I had always shared celebrations as our birthdays were just a week apart. We usually had joint drinks, but this year I couldn't face any sort of party. Instead I opted for afternoon tea in Soho where friends gave me gifts oriented towards foot protection for the impending trip. It was a lovely venue and so many people turned up but, as with any event since Jimmy died, I felt the need to get it over with. It didn't feel like something to be excited about and enjoyed. I wonder if that will ever come back?

Having managed to get up at 4am I get to Stansted airport and am informed by an impressively rude woman at the check-in desk that my luggage is over the limit weight-wise and I will have to either take stuff out or pay a fine. Because I didn't book the flight (and I would never actively choose this particular airline) it hadn't occurred to me that the allowance would be so small. I'm so tired and she's so obnoxious that I feel like giving up on the trip there and then. Instead I join the queue of despondent passengers who are paying through the nose for various misdemeanours that this airline seems to capitalise on in order to compensate for its cheap flights. When I get to Madrid I follow all the directions from the travel company, which are quite confusing to me, and miraculously I find the bus stop. I look around at the other people there waiting for the bus and see that many of them are walkers – how do I know? Because all of them have proper walking sticks, *all* of them! They also seem to be sporting very natty and obviously special walking trousers which look like they have a zip at the knee to turn them into shorts, paired with slick-looking, probably breathable, t-shirts. I've got a couple of pairs of M&S shorts and Primark tops. I now know I will look woefully out of place, despite the fleece and pac-a-mac. Just then one man standing a few yards away from me catches my eye. He is certainly not a walker, wearing as he does a very sharp black suit and beautifully polished, very expensive-looking shoes. I catch his olive-skinned profile as he chats on his mobile. He is seriously good-looking and as he turns I catch a flicker of white around his neck. Oh my God, literally, he's a priest! A genuine cool dude of the cloth. How very *Thorn Birds*. It lifts my spirits immensely. The bus to Leon pulls in and I take a seat by the window ready for the five-hour drive. I'm joined on the bus by more, perfectly kitted-out walkers and, yes, they too have sticks.

We arrive at Leon bus station and as the terminus empties I'm the only one standing there waiting for the driver who, according to my travel instructions, will meet me there. This proves far from straightforward and I worry once again at my ability to get halfway across Spain by foot when I can't seem to follow the most basic of instructions. I wander out on to the street and see a portly Spanish man standing by his car obviously waiting for someone and fortunately I happen to be just that person. It's a massive relief and before long I'm pulling up outside a very sweet little hotel that is set in a lovely traditional-looking square. It's only three storeys high and looks like it was once someone's grand home. The second floor has a wrought iron balcony stretching across with blooming window boxes dotted along it. Opposite is a very imposing church, which I learn is the Basilica of San Isadora and apparently houses the chalice of Dona Urraca – whoever she may be. After checking in I'm thinking I may pop over to the Basilica and find out more about Dona Urraca but instead opt for sitting in the last of the early evening sunshine to drink a delicious cold *cerveza*. I'm sure she wouldn't mind. I'm feeling completely and utterly shattered and more than a little anxious about the walk tomorrow. What if I get lost? I can't believe I've been so stupid as to think I could walk 200 miles in eleven days – and *without* sticks! Here I am once again in my life feeling like the outsider. Bugger, bugger, bugger.

I'd spent my somewhat unconventional childhood/ youth feeling that life was the party I just hadn't been invited to. I had always been on the outside looking in for as long as I could remember. I knew that other folk weren't thinking the same things as me or worrying in the same way I did. I know I was happy until I was around seven and then the lovely aunt we lived with, who had taken Mum in when she was pregnant with me, died and everything went tits up after that. I'll just refer to what happened to me when I was nine as the 'event' as I really don't want to descend into *mis-lit*, but suffice to say it took away my childhood and introduced me to shame. My bereavement counsellor told me that many grieving people experience 'imposter' syndrome, wherein you feel you are in the crowd but don't feel worthy of being there. But I had felt that way my whole life. That is, until I met Jimmy. He made me feel I was on life's Guest List. 'Good to see you, Claire, you're looking great tonight, come in and have a free cocktail! We've been waiting for you'…

I try to shake off these miserable thoughts; after all, I'm in Spain! I love Spain, so did Jimmy. He loved the way that the modernist architecture sits so comfortably with the classic. I'm in the land that spawned the adventurous, innovative minds of Picasso, Miro, Gaudi, Dali, Cervantes and Lorca. I miss Jimmy so much as I sip my beer and read up about Leon. This feeling intensifies as I read that trout fishing is particularly good in this area and the flies are of 'artisan quality'. Jimmy loved trout- and fly-fishing. If I couldn't sleep he would lull me off by recounting the spawning patterns of river and sea trout – he was endlessly incredulous as to why some chose rivers and some chose the great oceans. And when he got his collection of flies out he was in heaven, describing just which flies were for which season and which fish. I would look at him lovingly and say 'I don't think it's possible I could be more bored'.

He would also have loved the fact that the Spanish still smoke wantonly. They love it. It's not a class thing, just a Spanish thing. Having myself recently stopped smoking and therefore having the olfactory sense of a truffle pig, when I got on the bus in Madrid I could immediately smell the smokers who had obviously stubbed out their last fix for the five-hour trip. As we disembarked at Leon there was a cluster at the starting gate with fag in fingers ready for a light as soon as they hit the tarmac. Jimmy could wax lyrical about the various brands of cigarettes he'd smoked over the years; we'd talked about him writing a book about it as a history of his life, it would have been funny. Of course he had the good sense to give up but always missed it.

The worst thing, I realised, about Jimmy dying was the loss of that secure bubble I had existed in. I had no doubt how much I loved him and how much he loved me. It was a daily given. He would wake up, look at me and ask me what it was like to be beautiful (trust me, I'm not!). I would then cross my eyes at him – he would always laugh. Next he'd ask me if I wanted tea and what kind? Proper tea? To which (and trust me, this was every morning) I would reply 'all proper tea is theft' – I know, but it never got tired to us. Then, the secure sounds of Jimmy feeding cats downstairs and boiling the kettle, the sound of him coming upstairs, putting one cup down on the landing while he opened our door. And then the chat over tea as we planned our day. It was immediately after he died that I realised this would never happen, ever again. That everyday, mundane ritual that I adored was gone from my life.

I don't mind being in Leon on my own one bit, but it's so bizarre to be far away and not be calling or emailing Jimmy. When you are so close to another person you find that you look at life differently, you take into account their views and it forms the prism through which you view the world. So as well as your own response to things, there's always the thought of what the other person would think. And, inevitably, the excitement to then share and discuss with them. However, there is something quite liberating, if not a little scary, about the fact that nobody knows where I am or where I will be. No one asked for a copy of my itinerary (and why should they?) so I'm here but no one but me knows where. I like it – sort of.

I dig out the plastic wallet with all my information from the travel company in and read the description of what to expect from the walk tomorrow. I know it's quite an easy one to start with. I read through it a week ago and as far as I can see Thursday is the tough day, uphill for around eight hours, which makes me really quite nervous. But that's Thursday and today's Saturday. I must live more in the moment or at least just take a look at tomorrow's itinerary. The funny thing is, I think my main worry about the walk, aside from not looking the part and not having sticks, is whether I'll find toilets! I'm sure they don't have *Camino cabanas* along the route. It's such a British thing to be fussing about. Och, as they say in Scotland, we'll see.

I'm sent to eat dinner in a small restaurant nearby as the hotel doesn't serve food. The meal isn't great, some dry fish and over-boiled vegetables. It's disappointing as I love Spanish food; I hope this isn't a foretaste of what to expect cuisine-wise. I go back to the hotel intending to turn in for the night but it's quite lively and there's some sort of show going on in what looks like a disco area by the bar. I'm intrigued. The hotel has entertainment laid on for the guests in the form of a Spanish boy band and I end up staying far later than I should, especially given that I was up so early this morning. Despite it being so jolly I know this is no way to prep for my first day of a 300-kilometres-plus walk tomorrow so I reluctantly leave the *muchachos* to their fun and hit the sack before I'm tempted to get up and dance.

Day 1 - Trek Summary
Hospital de Orbigo to Astorga

A driver will collect you from your hotel in Leon and drive you to Hospital de Orbigo to start your trek. The multi-arched Gothic bridge from where you set off was originally constructed in the thirteenth century and remains the most famous along the Camino. From here a reasonably easy day lies ahead with the Camino passing through forests and long easy tracks with good views.

Time: 4 hours
Ascent: 140 metres
Descent: 90 metres
Distance: 17 kilometres

CHAPTER 3

TO BE A PILGRIM

'He who would valiant be, 'gainst all disaster.
Let him in constancy follow the master.
There's no discouragement can make him once relent,
His first avowed intent,
To be a pilgrim.'

I go to bed on Saturday night a widow, I awake on Sunday morning a pilgrim (or *peregrino*) ready to change my life one step at a time, or at least that was the plan. However, this pilgrim needed to be extremely valiant on her first morning as disaster struck in a right royal fashion.

Being anal I love nothing better than a 'to do' list and a perfectly worked-out plan. I used to put together intricate itineraries for Jimmy and me when we'd go on a trip. So I'd planned for my first morning to be an exercise in well-ordered serenity. Wake up at 7am according to my phone (that's UK time so it's really 6am – great). I set the alarm to give myself a lie-in but still allow me an hour to decide which shoes to wear. I have a choice of three varieties of footwear that I plan to rotate and hopefully avoid blisters: my walking boots, a pair of trainers and a most ugly pair of walking sandals (they involve Velcro – ugh). I plan to wash and blow dry my hair, have a leisurely breakfast, collect my picnic lunch and, most importantly, collect my 'passport'.

I'm very excited about the passport as to me it's the most important element of the trip; it's what makes it more than just a long walk. They look like the old cardboard passports you used to be able to get for a year in the UK back in the 70s and each pilgrim is issued with one. I've read that you need to obtain a minimum of two stamps (or *sellos*) per day as you walk. Nearly all the cafés and churches have a unique stamp and the idea is that at the end of the walk, in Santiago, you hand over your passport full of stamps and get a certificate. You then attend the Pilgrims' Mass in the cathedral that houses the remains of St James (or Santiago as he's known here). I imagine this will be like a massive graduation ceremony – I can't wait. And obviously getting the passport at the beginning is an absolute *must*.

I'm woken by a ringing that leaves me completely confused: my mobile's alarm doesn't sound like a phone ringing – what's going on? And then I realise that's because it's not my mobile, it's the hotel phone right by my bed. Hmm, no one knows I'm here, so what's this? I'll tell you what it is – it's reception telling me that my driver has arrived and is waiting for me. WHAT?!!! How can that be? And suddenly I realise I've had a completely blonde episode. Instead of putting the clock forward I've put it back. Shit, shit, shit – I fly out of bed and pull on the pair of sweat pants that are nearest, a t-shirt and the ugly walking sandals – Velcro may well be ugly but by golly it's quick. I chuck stuff unceremoniously into my suitcase, pull a brush through my hair and fly downstairs gagging for a coffee.

While the driver's putting my bags in the car I run over to get my picnic lunch and manage to swig down a *café con leche*. I'm feeling completely stressed, plus the weather is terrible, thick grey clouds. It doesn't feel right starting the walk in these circumstances but I figure I'll just get my passport and get on the road. But even this isn't straightforward. The gorgeous young girl at reception doesn't speak very good English and my Spanish is pretty appalling. I finally get her to understand that I want a passport and that according to my paperwork there will be one waiting for me, but she has none, only a rubber stamp from the hotel. I'm standing by the people-carrier with my driver waiting patiently trying desperately to make the gorgeous one understand that I *have* to have a passport, I really do, when a few drops of rain begin to fall.

And just like that something clicks in my brain and I find myself mentally stamping my feet and screaming internally 'NO! NO! NO!' and then to everyone's surprise (especially mine) I start to cry. Not an angry, frustrated glistening of tears in the eyes, but full-on sobs, so much that I can't speak. There's no going back once you've shown your hand and started to cry. You can't say 'oh no, I was just joking' or 'you were mistaken'. It's all over once the tears start to roll and the more sympathy you get the more you cry. I realise there's only one thing to do in this situation – well it's obvious – I tell them I'm a widow. Only they don't really understand. The driver pats my shoulders and I break into a mime by way of an attempted explanation. I point at Jimmy's wedding ring that I'm sporting alongside my own wedding ring and engagement ring on my left hand. And I'm pretty sure I performed the international symbol of death by pulling my finger across my throat. To be fair they were very good about it, but then the Latins don't blanche at hysteria like us Brits. The gorgeous one pats my back and stamps the *sellos* from the hotel onto a piece of paper and mimes that I can stick that into my passport, whenever I get it. I nod by way of acceptance, wipe my nose on the back of my hand, get into the people-carrier and snap on sunglasses despite the rain. The driver doesn't say a word during the journey but I sense his quiet sympathy and it comforts me.

He drops me at Hospital de Orbigo right by the Roman bridge I've read about, and it is beautiful. My previous sense of despair is instantly replaced by delight at starting my adventure in such an apposite way. Having studied ancient myths and read *The Hero with a Thousand Faces* by the master of mythology Joseph Campbell, I am only too aware of the symbolic significance of a hero beginning his or her journey by crossing water. And as soon as I cross into the quaint village I feel calm and ready for anything, including the rain – after all I have a pac-a-mac. I dive into a café and restart my day with a coffee and a croissant but I have to admit feeling a slight twinge of envy as several pilgrims stamp their passports at the counter before collecting their bloody sticks and heading out on the road. I decide that due to my lack of the Germanic-looking walking aids I shall adopt a churlish disdain towards them. In fact I will go as far as to say I think in many ways sticks are a form of cheating. Who needs 'em?

My previous fear of getting lost is dispelled as I see there are plenty of yellow arrows along the route, some official but many looking like they've been helpfully spray-painted by my predecessors on the roads and walls of villages we pass through. I look up at the sky and see there is enough blue to make a sailor a pair of pants (as my mother would say). Before long the sun comes out and I find myself walking alone through the fields as the temperature rises. It is glorious

– until I remember I omitted to apply sunscreen due to the earlier rainy weather and my rushed departure from Leon, and my bottle of factor 50 is now sitting in my suitcase being transported to the next town.

I notice that I seem to be walking slightly faster than the other folk on the road and am regularly overtaking them. I hope that's ok. I'm not sure if there's some sort of Camino etiquette I'm breaking. I know it's not a race but I've always found walking slowly really difficult. I had to really work at it when I was with Jimmy. He loved to be out and about and when we were first together he would take me walking in Edinburgh and was able to get to the top of a relatively steep hill. But latterly he would be out of puff walking on streets that you and I would probably think were quite flat.

I enter a wooded area, which is also symbolic for a hero on his journey. And I ponder the fact that I am doing this walk in twelve days and that's an auspicious number. Campbell breaks the mythological journey into twelve stages so I've unwittingly created my own myth. There are yellow arrows on trees whose shade I'm enjoying as the sun is now high in the sky and it's *scorchio*. The Camino symbol is also a bright yellow sea shell and is beautiful. I've always loved the colour yellow and when I was little I realised that yellow was the most important colour of all. I would get a new set of colouring pencils and loved they way they were laid out in the tin in order of shade and tone and looked so very cheerful, but I found that if you took out the yellow pencil the other colours became somehow duller, less confident in their cheer. Put the yellow back and they instantly become vibrant, full of potential, alive. Jimmy was my yellow pencil.

I haven't looked at my watch as it really doesn't matter what time it is. If I'm thirsty I'll drink, if I'm hungry I'll eat, simple as that. Before I know it I'm climbing a steep hill and as I reach the top I see the City of Astorga in the distance looking very dramatic with a stunning cathedral proudly sitting in the midst of the houses. It's a lovely moment and I take the time to stand and stare. And in that moment I get it completely. I know that I am doing exactly the right thing at the right time; it's rare in life that you get such a feeling. I had it once before standing up in the back of a cattle truck travelling through Cuba (but that's another story). If parallel worlds do exist I am convinced that whatever my 'other' self does in these worlds, at some point she would be taking this walk, I have no doubt whatsoever of that fact; even in my sliding-doors life I would be here. As I trot into the city a very smartly dressed Spanish woman passes me and with a sunshine smile wishes me a *buen Camino* – that's me! I'm on the Camino and she wants me to have a *buen* one.

When I arrive at my hotel I see my suitcase in the reception amid other bags being transported (I note that it looks to be one of the biggest ones there) and the receptionist seems to be fully expecting me as she immediately hands me my passport. I figure she's liaised with the receptionist in Leon as she looks at me with some trepidation as if to say 'please don't cry all over my reception'. I look at all the squares ready to be stamped and she does me the honour of sticking the stamp from Leon carefully in the front and then stamping the personalised hotel *sellos* into the first empty white square next to it. I couldn't be happier, and after a blissful bath and hair wash I head out to find an *albergue* in order to get another stamp. The *albergues* are sort of youth hostels for the pilgrims, with dormitories and communal kitchens. All a bit too hippy for me, but there's a warm atmosphere, and as I offer the woman at the desk money for a stamp she flashes a huge grin and says 'stamps and smiles are still free here'. I love hippies.

My hotel is actually quite fancy with a grand wood-panelled dining room and my room overlooks the cathedral. Dinner is lovely and I'm given a tasty bottle of local chilled red wine but can only manage one glass as I realize I am well and truly cream-crackered. There are a few other *peregrinos* dining and I'm very glad I'm alone with my thoughts as I can overhear one woman boring the arse off of another about her reasons for walking; she doesn't let the other get a word in edgewise. I happily hit the sack and am grateful for the earplugs I threw in my case as an afterthought. The price of a cathedral view is that I also get the clock chiming on the hour and half hour. I kiss my photo of Jimmy before sinking into blackness.

Day 2 - Trek Summary
Astorga to Rabanal del Camino

Another easy-going day with the Camino
passing over wide open stretches (take care
if hot). At Valdeviejas it is possible to take
a short detour to the beautifully restored
Maragato village of Castrillo de los Povazares.

Time: 4.4 hours
Ascent: 256 metres
Descent: 30 metres
Distance: 21½ kilometres

CHAPTER 4

FITTING THE BILL

This morning could not be more different to yesterday. I wake up to my alarm and have a long shower, leisurely breakfast and time to select my outfit and try out the anti-blister spray (one of my birthday gifts); I figure it's worth a go. I don a pair of my new walking socks and walking boots. A wee word about the latter footwear. I was asked by so many people before I came on the walk whether I had an old pair of boots as if the age made them somehow more effective protection. Of course I replied 'yes' as they were indeed purchased over five years ago. I omitted to mention that they had only had two outings since being bought and those were dog-walking a friend's mutt in a muddy field so hardly a proper road-test. Checking out my image in the mirror with shorts and my new fleece I have to say I do rather look the part.

Just so you get the picture, I have very developed calf muscles – they're actually due to an obscure muscular condition I have (Thomsen's Disease if you're interested) and are something of a paradox as I wasn't able to participate in a lot of sports at school although I look like I should be winning a gold in the 100 metres. Usually I detest them as they are so very unfeminine, in my opinion, but today they come into their own. I'm not boasting when I say I could be a strong contender for Miss September if there was a Camino de Santiago calendar. I may never wear a pair of skinny jeans but I'm getting envious looks from the cyclists gearing up to head off outside the hotel.

I leave my suitcase in reception and I'm off, turning left at the cathedral as instructed by my guidebook, and soon I'm heading out of town following the now familiar yellow arrows. The sky is quite grey – Jimmy would have described it as 'mackerel' in one of his scripts – but over to the west there is a small village throwing out a quarter of a beautiful rainbow. I notice that there are stone markers telling the distance to Santiago which have the yellow seashell but also a quarter of a rainbow, it's so poetic. Everyone loves a rainbow; they are such a natural gift. It's like Mother Nature, having created rain and snow and sunshine, asked her child what it would like to add and it came up with a rainbow for no other reason than it looks so pretty.

I love the walk today and find I have the most enormous appetite (my mum would have said 'you've lost your appetite and found a donkey's') and despite having had a good breakfast I stop and grab another croissant and coffee in a café about an hour in. Overtaking more pilgrims, I'm alone again in an open field and my internal jukebox is playing a Nirvana song but instead of the line 'love myself better than you' I find I'm singing 'love my fleece…' Who knew that a hitherto despised sartorial choice would now be my best friend as it's become quite windy? Jimmy would really laugh at this as we joked about how my clothing choices when we lived in Edinburgh bore little or no reference to the weather. I just couldn't reconcile my wardrobe to the climate in summer and would often be frozen by the biting easterly winds. He would chuckle as we left our flat with him sporting a thick sweater and massive warm coat and I'd present myself completely inadequately dressed. I always said I'd rather freeze than be seen in a fleece and here I was not only wearing one but having a growing affection for it. Just to make it clear though, I will still never be seen in Birkenstocks no matter how comfortable folk say they are.

I'm starting to recognise familiar faces on the Camino and am now quite happy to *buen Camino* those I pass. I still can't seem to pace myself and hope this doesn't catch up on me; I don't want to 'peak' too early in the journey. In an outside café in a tiny village I stop to eat once more and the female owner offers me, of all things, a whisky! I wonder what that's all about. I settle for water and a delicious tuna tortilla. I can't believe how famished I am. In walk a German couple who sit in the direct bright sunlight and order two large beers. I can't imagine drinking them and then walking in this heat. I'm quietly impressed.

Having asked for my *sellos* the owner's six-year-old daughter does the honours and brings out the ink pad with the stamp placed on top and treads carefully with it held out in front of her as if serving at the altar. I love kids and they seem to like me. In my sliding-doors life Jimmy and I were planning to get IVF even with my advancing years. I'd miscarried two years previously and we'd been hugely disappointed so this would have been my last throw of the dice to experience parenthood. How would that have panned out? I think about how I would have part of him still here with me now. The girl comes closer and I can tell she is checking me out as she ceremoniously stamps my passport. I must have passed the test as before long she comes out sporting coloured pencils and two pieces of clean white paper. She places her hand on the back of a plastic chair and gives me the international expression for 'is it ok to join you?' and I respond with the downward mouth movement combined with a shrug of the shoulder and lift of both eyebrows to signify 'can't see why not'. I draw the only two things I'm any good at (and these, trust me, are not great): a cat and a rabbit. And then because I knew the Spanish for 'house' I rustle her up a *casa* for good measure. She goes back into the kitchen and reappears with a board game; I've obviously passed the drawing test and she is ready to upgrade the relationship to a Spanish board version of the card game 'Beggar my Neighbour'. But I have a Camino to conquer and regretfully shake my head, pay up and hit the road. I think she understands.

I am slightly concerned that my right knee is feeling sore and there's a pain in my lower back when I descend the steeper slopes and is that a blister I'm feeling on the back of my right heel? The well-meaning words of friends who were advising some sort of training regime prior to the walk echo in my ears but just for a few minutes. Sod it! Deep breath and onward.

The villages I walk through are getting further apart and smaller, more rustic, and are thoroughly enchanting. I meander the open vistas and, having opted not to have any earphones interfering with my experience, decide instead to sing. Hmm, what should I select from my repertoire? I want something to sustain me for a while and as I enter a vineyard settle on *Joseph and his Amazing Technicolour Dreamcoat*, although I can never remember all the colours and I'm not even entirely sure what ochre actually is. 'It was red and yellow and green and hmm and hmm and ochre and hmm and blue…' It's a bit of a harsh story when you think about it. There you are, a happy farming family, and just because your wee brother gets a fancy new coat you decide to commit fratricide. Couldn't they just nick it and sell it? I don't think I'd be able to forgive them and share out my corn years later when I became king. I'd let the jealous bastards starve.

There's something very liberating about this walk and I can feel a real energy emanating from the Camino: the ghosts of the thousands of pilgrims who preceded me? I love the idea that I can walk across a country and all I have to do is get up in the morning, get breakfast and head off, nothing more to consider than the basics. It couldn't be further from my day-to-day life these past ten months. No making beds, no unpacking dishwashers, no washing clothes. And, most importantly, no opening endless letters with the heading 'the Estate of James Gardner'. I hate these more than the sympathy cards. They are so cold and yet there's an irony in the grandness of the word 'Estate'. It makes it sound like I've been left Downton Abbey when the reality is I've been left with a bunch of debts and am for the first time in my life having to navigate the UK benefits system.

'...Bring me my coloured coat, my amaaaaazzzing, cooolooooreeed coooooooat.' The curtain goes down on my fine performance as I enter the tiny village of Rabanal, which seems to be solely populated with fellow *peregrinos*, and I'm starting to recognise folk which I suppose is inevitable. I'm looking forward to the longer days, I like the idea of arriving in town early evening having walked seven or eight hours. Rabanal is utterly charming. Rustic stone buildings with ancient-looking wooden balconies hanging over the cobbled streets. The hotel is tiny and gorgeous. I have a welcome shower and discover my first blister, a badge of honour, I feel, but it doesn't really hurt and I figure I'll change footwear tomorrow as part of my rotation plan. Dinner's not til 8.30pm so I decide on a wee nap in my attic room and I am awoken by church bells around 7.00pm. I feel compelled to head over to the church, figuring it must be some sort of call to mass. I follow the locals and enter the cave-like place of worship and I'm right, it's a pilgrim's mass. To my surprise a dead ringer for Forest Whitaker comes out in ceremonial robes and asks an Englishwoman in the congregation to read a piece from the bible. Then we wait and two other priests turn up and there's no denying what Jimmy's grandmother used to say – the Catholics put on a good show.

I'm actually technically Jewish having converted in my mid-20s when I married my first Jewish-American husband. I love all the traditions and storytelling and particularly I love their dark irreverent humour. One lunch meeting Jimmy and I had in Glasgow he offered to buy me a pastrami sandwich and was quite shocked when I quoted my ex-husband's family's comment that 'pastrami killed more Jews than Hitler'. There's another story I think is hilarious even if it may be apocryphal; there was a stage production of *The Diary of Anne Frank* in Los Angeles. It was so dire that when the Nazis came on stage looking for the hidden family the audience shouted out 'they're upstairs'. It did make me chuckle. My mum was Catholic and when I converted she was just happy that I had at least one Testament under my belt.

The priest finishes off the service by blessing the pilgrims and splashing us with holy water. It's interesting the diversity of the congregation. There are a couple of very young-look-ing pilgrims, maybe in their early twenties, as well as the little old Spanish local ladies who have appeared for their daily worship. A woman I recognise from the walk today spoils the moment by filming the event on her camera?! The priest has to ask her to stop. She doesn't seem embarrassed in the slightest and shamelessly pops the camera back in her rucksack.

Back at the hotel I sip a beer while writing before dinner. I bought a notebook before I left the UK with a classic Penguin cover of Jack Kerouac's *On the Road* – it felt fitting. Writing has become an integral part of my day as I've found I really need to do a sort of mind-dump after being with my thoughts; it's like emptying the bag of a vacuum cleaner ready to fill up again the next day. The barman comes over with a plate of complimentary tapas and tells me I am Cervantes – that makes me happy; perhaps I won't even tell him I'm a widow but of course I can't help myself.

At dinner I'm on the next table to the boring woman from last night. She's found a new victim and speaks loudly in English and again barely stops to draw breath. She tells how her daughter won't speak to her anymore; you kind of feel some sympathy for the daughter. The food in the hotel is really good. I eat eel, it's delicious. I've loved it since I was a young child and we practised the true Cockney tradition of having jellied eels for Sunday tea. I didn't really understand what they were back then and thought they were called 'deels' as in jelly deels so never connected them to the slippery water snake. Although what I thought 'deels' were I can't tell you. Jimmy was so shocked when I first ordered them in the trendy Chop House restaurant in Clerkenwell. The venue has them etched on the smoked-glass window but that's more for authenticity and by now is probably meant to be ironic. The Polish waitress couldn't hide her look of disgust and incredulity as if this was the first time she'd actually been asked for them … maybe it was! Jimmy said that it was at this point he realised I was in fact a true Londoner (I think he really meant that I was common!).

I miss Jimmy a lot today, especially now I'm people-watching – our favourite activity. I feel a little heavy-hearted as I climb to my little room at the top of the hotel but am too tired to get morose. As Scarlett O'Hara would say, 'tomorrow is another day'.

Day 3 - Trek Summary
Rabanal del Camino to Molinaseca

A glorious but more challenging day as the Camino climbs to its highest point in the Cordillera Cantabrica with far-reaching views. The route passes through many quiet pretty villages.

Average Time: 5¾ hours
Ascent: 504 metres
Descent: 900 metres
Distance: 26½ kilometres

CHAPTER 5

THREE IS THE
MAGIC NUMBER

My mum always used to tell me 'plodders get places'. I'm pretty certain she meant it in a positive way as in (said in an American accent) 'Kid. You and me are going places.' And here I am decades on, my mum no longer gracing us with her presence (breast cancer took her in 1996), and I am indeed plodding but just what 'place' am I heading to? If I can get to *me* that would be a good start. I'd lost that *me* when Jimmy died. After my overdose, I had hit my nadir, surely it couldn't get worse, couldn't hurt more? I'd had to go to Lewisham A&E where the receptionist asked me who my next of kin was and I burst into tears – did I have a next of kin? I sat with Pia and Deb, two saints of friends who stayed at the hospital all day with me, crying non-stop. I really didn't care that I was sitting in a busy public area. In the midst of the tears and snot it hit me all of a sudden; as much as I missed Jimmy, I missed Claire. I missed 'us' but I also missed the person

I had been with him. I can't imagine finding that girl ever again. Among some of the most bizarre comments some folk proffered by way of words of comfort, one of the strangest was having it pointed it out to me that I was on my own for quite a few years before meeting Jimmy so surely I could just return to that way of life. I think of the song lyrics – 'if I hadn't seen such riches I could live with being poor'. I can't go back, and more importantly I don't want to go back, but I do want to stop feeling so insignificant and invisible, I do want to reconnect with the me that was forty-odd years in the making and has now somehow left the building. It's very lonely without her. Maybe plodding will be a start to the search to get her back. I always hated the expression 'to find oneself' but I have to acknowledge that for me it has become essential. I need to stop being an outline of a person.

It's day three and I like the number three very much. There's the three-act structure I love in drama, there's those three little words and now I feel in many ways that I'm in my third stage of grief. I know there's some psychological structure outlining the stages of grief, something like denial, anger, depression blah, blah and then acceptance. It's great to try to tidy up the process but it's not that simple, it really isn't, at least it's not for me. My personal stages of grief go like this (and in my head I compare them with those pictures you see of early mankind). Stage 1 I'm on my hands and knees, post-funeral – pre-suicide attempt. Then having decided to stick around I get to stage 2 and became bi-pedal again, just about standing upright. But I'm still in complete darkness in terms of seeing any kind of tomorrow, this Neanderthal me hasn't discovered fire yet to light the black and warm my soul. At best I can tentatively put one foot in front of the other in the blackness and hope that the road will rise up to meet me. I understand two concepts fully now, the first being utter despair and the second being blind faith.

I am ravenous when I wake this morning and my toast and jam and *café con leche* feel like a feast. I go back to my room and dress for the road and drag my suitcase down to reception. If the other cases are village houses, mine is the Empire State – it's huge and really stands out among the other modest bags. I feel slightly embarrassed. As I'm about to leave the hotel I catch sight of myself in the full-length mirror by the entrance. In contrast to yesterday's 'looking the part', this morning I pulled on a vest top and forgot to put on a bra (now in the mammoth suitcase in reception). The top is quite short and, as I have no belt holding up my denim cut-off jeans, leaves a slight gap. Rather than walking shoes, I've changed to trainers to help the new blister. With newly washed hair left loose the overall look is, well, frankly, quite slutty. I might well still be a contender for a Camino calendar but one of a very different sort, probably involving me being hosed down with water prior to the photo shoot. 'Och well, too late now,' I think, and head out into the sunshine.

As I mentioned earlier, I wear Jimmy's wedding ring on my ring finger next to my wedding ring and engagement ring; it's quite bulky but having taken his ring off his finger straight after he died I cannot bear to be parted from it. One of the first things I did was to get it altered to fit my ring finger. However, I've now discovered that the walk and the heat conspire to give me quite horrible sausage fingers. I got quite scared yesterday that they would get so large that I wouldn't be able to get the rings off at all and had visions of me visiting a local hospital to have them (or my fingers) cut off. I took the rings off and sport them round my neck on a chain I wear which does the job for now. I suspect that I'm not drinking enough water so aim to up my intake but then I'll need the loo more – it's a balancing act I need to figure out.

I really hadn't expected the hugely beautiful walk today. Incredible scenery as the Camino climbs to its highest point in the magically named Cordillera Cantabrica. The views are staggering and villages heartbreakingly lovely. I am completely bowled over. What was it Wordsworth wittered on about amidst his daffodils? Something about 'a poet could not but be gay in such a jocund company'. And jocund indeed is the company. The folk en route today seem to be quite a game bunch. I pass one group (yes, I'm still passing people) consisting of five Spanish guys who look more like they are on a stag weekend in Amsterdam than a spiritual pilgrimage. They are hilarious. It is 10.30am and they are passing round one of those Spanish skin wine holders – I seem to remember it being a thing on Spanish holidays in the 1970s to have sangria poured into open-mouthed parents from such containers from a couple of feet in the air. As I pass they offer it to me. That's the second day I've been offered booze on the walk; who knew? To be fair to them, given my attire, I probably look well up-for-it. I politely refuse, '*buen camino*' them and trot off up a hill trying not to jiggle my unsupported chest too much.

About half an hour later I find myself trekking through the heather as outlined in my guide, the bonny bonny heather, and I realise that I need to go to the loo really badly. Checking my guide, I figure it will be at least an hour until I reach an appropriate facility. What to do? I'd thought a lot about this prior to the trip. Despite the incredibly comprehensive travel documents, nothing outlined the Camino etiquette for getting caught short. I am on a remote track with woodland either side, I passed a couple of German girls some time back and a real plodder is up ahead of me. There is nothing for it; I join the bear fraternity in woodland usage. There really is a first time for everything. I can change the expression now to 'does a Claire ... in a wood?' and the answer is yes, she absolutely does.

Now I feel at this juncture I need to make a huge confession to you. I know you are probably thinking that the previous revelation is quite enough for one day but this is different. This is really quite serious. Brace yourself. Today I walked using sticks! I know, I know, but I bought them before I left Astorga and I couldn't bring myself to tell you. It was a bit of an accident really. I had headed out straight after breakfast hoping to find that the *zapateria* that I'd discovered last night on my stroll through the town would be open as I'd spotted a very cute pair of kitten-heeled slingbacks on sale in the window that had my name written all over them. But unfortunately it was shut and instead I passed a pilgrim shop selling among other things the erstwhile offensive items and something clicked, it was now or never. A voice in my head was saying 'buy the sticks, Claire'. They cost the same as the bloody shoes! So today I road-tested them knowing I would be navigating some steep ascents and descents in the mountains and I'm a convert! Hallelujah and all hail to the walking sticks. I love them, I love them more than my fleece, they are brilliant, what was I thinking? I take it all back. The pain in my right knee? Gone. The sore lower back? Disappeared. I descend the steep slopes leaning forward with the sticks doing all the work looking like a crazy, slutty insect. It's great. What were you thinking trying to put me off buying them? Are you crazy? Give me a break, don't you know I'm a widow?

After the most beautiful walk through the mountains, I descend into Molinaseca, a stunning village with a river running through, it and I'm delighted to discover that my hotel room overlooks this. I arrive around 3.30pm, so a slightly longer day today. I know now that the walk is going to get tougher in the coming days. And I've been nervously looking ahead in my guidebook to day six, which starts with 'for most pilgrims, this day is very tough indeed'. But that's not for a couple of days. Tomorrow is seven and a quarter hours according to the guidebook. My well-developed calves got burnt today so out with the factor 50 tomorrow. No sausage fingers today though – was that due to the wonderful sticks? Ah, the sticks…

Day 4 - Trek Summary
Molinaseca to Villafranca del Bierzo

A long day of steady walking with minimal ascents and descents. The first half of the day is through Ponferrada and suburbs but the terrain and scenery improve as the day progresses ending with a delightful walk through vineyards to your much-needed resting place of Villafranca del Bierzo.

Average Time: 7¼ hours
Ascent: 140 metres
Descent: 250 metres
Distance: 32½ kilometres

CHAPTER 6

PILGRIM PALS

The screenwriting and storytelling guru Robert McKee stated in his three-day seminar that the person in a relationship who first says 'I love you' loses power. It's a cynical view and possibly more reflective of Mr McKee's relationships. Jimmy told me he loved me very early on in our relationship. As I mentioned earlier, we'd met a couple of years prior to getting together and got to know and like each other immensely. I was his script editor on a TV show he was writing, an adaptation of a Swedish crime novel (what, I hear you say, Swedish crime dramas? They'll never catch on!), and although there were the usual issues with the script (adaptations are notoriously tricky buggers to write), the huge saving grace was us hanging out together having script meetings. As I said, he used to disappear at times so one time I chased him down and flew over from Glasgow to Derry to give him notes. I remember back then we took time out of the script work to drive round the beautiful Irish countryside and a tiny voice at the back of my head said 'well now, this almost feels like a date' but I put that out of my mind in a 'No, it's Jimmy. Jimmy Gardner the writer. Don't be so soft'-type way. I smiled at his declaration of love, wine had been taken, but he hadn't said it for a reciprocal response – just as well. He also suggested marriage within the first two months of being together. Bearing in mind that he'd made it to his late 40s without any form of matrimony and I had two under my belt, this did make me chuckle. I told him that according to psychologists, men are more likely to propose in the first three months of a relationship – in the 'first flush' period. So he waited exactly one week after we'd been together three months and asked me again. I still said no but over the coming years he persuaded me it would be a good idea. He was right, it was.

I set off walking at 9am after my coffee and toast. Although I'm tempted by the croissants that are also on offer, I decide, this time, not to be greedy. The first hour or so is quite boring but then I hit the beautiful town of Ponferrada. It's bigger than the previous villages I've encountered, and hiking up to the main square and its bustling cafés I realise I am ready for another breakfast. I find a table in the sunshine and as I give my order discover they have run out of croissants – I knew I'd regret leaving that one at the hotel.

I'm sitting next to two young women, one of them polishing off a croissant. They've heard me order and so know that I'm English. One of them, Hannah, asks where I'm from. She's an American and as we start talking I realise it is so very odd to be having a conversation involving more than ordering food and drink. She and Victoria (an Italian) have been walking for two and a half weeks, right from the start of the Camino in France. They are doing the whole hardcore *albergue* deal, carrying their lives in rucksacks. I feel a little shameful with my small rucksack and knowledge of my big suitcase being transported to the next destination.

Hannah is a photographer and so is also carrying an impressive, huge camera. She has a lovely face to match her warm personality and we swap life stories and now that I've started talking I find I can't stop. Hannah takes my phone number as she says they all muck in and cook at the *albergues* and I should go over one night as we are following the same route and will be in roughly the same villages over the coming days. Victoria is only 23 – I realise I could easily be her mother – and beautiful in that way only Italians can be. Hannah tells me tales of life on the 'proper' Camino (my choice of words not hers), which does sound quite gruelling. The *albergues* are pretty basic hostel accommodation and sharing with other pilgrims sounds challenging. I realise that as well as the nifty footwear rotation I've got going, one other reason I'm not suffering with awful blisters is that I'm not carrying the weight of a donkey on my back.

I love chatting with them but as I get back on my way I figure that this is about being with me and my thoughts and feelings rather than hooking up with new people or making new friends. However, in terms of my relationship with grief, I'd say it is now moving to the side a little and allowing me some space to engage with new folk and have new experiences (dare I say move forward? Maybe I won't go as far as that). I'm thinking that I'll check what day Hannah 'graduates' in Santiago and if it's at the same time as me then we could get dinner. I have never graduated from anything in my life, having been thrown out of secretarial college at the age of 19 and being told I wouldn't amount to much. It wasn't for anything dramatic unfortunately, I just didn't go to class enough as I found it incredibly boring and had a boyfriend in a band and preferred staying out late attending his gigs to learning standard shorthand. However, to this day I have to say I still use my antiquated shorthand skills and can touch type, so not all wasted. As I mentioned previously, I see the end of the walk as constituting a graduation – I'll get a pilgrim's certificate (or *Compostela*) and the mass at the cathedral will be the ceremony (I hear that they read out your name). I've even packed a dress and shoes for the occasion – no fleece or sticks on that day.

Back on the walk again and already I'm ravenous – well, I had expected a croissant at the previous stop. I thought I might lose weight on the walk but actually I find I'm stuffing my face like nobody's business and there seem to be a lot of carbs involved. I resolve to opt for salads from now on. I enter a tiny village called Fuentes Nueves. My guidebook tells me there are three cafés, I see the first one but decide not to stop as I usually would and instead end up at the third, which turns out to be a cracker. Not wanting bread, but hankering after more than iceberg lettuce and tinned tuna, I figure I'll branch out to a *tortilla con queso* (cheese omelette to you and me). However, our wires get crossed and the lovely woman who owns the place comes out with the hugest omelette ever. There must be at least five eggs in it and it comes inside a massive baguette. So much for no carbs. I wait until she's out of sight and I'm sitting alone outside and pick up the bread, wrap it in serviettes and shove it in my backpack – I'll give it to the birds later – and devour every bit of the delicious omelette.

The problem with walking due west is that during the early part of the day the sun is on your back and then for a huge chunk on your left side. It's not conducive to an all-over tan and I can feel the side of my left calf is smarting so decide to stop again quite soon for a coffee and some shade and to get a stamp. I sit outside where there are a couple of tables by the dusty roadside. And then I see a sight to throw me back in time. Out comes a little girl of about 6 or 7 with a man who looks to be her grandfather. They cross the road and he lets her into his battered old Volvo, blessing her in Spanish as she sneezes twice. He is completely attentive and treats her sneeze as though it's potentially life-threatening and this makes me smile. He then walks over to the driver's door and gets in. I realise he hasn't put a seat belt on the wee girl and she's sitting in the front of the car. Before firing up the engine he fires up a filterless cigarette and takes care to shut all the windows before driving off – himself also seatbeltless. It resembles a scene straight out of my 1970s childhood. I wonder if he has an eight-track playing the Spanish equivalent of 'Crackling Rosie'. Ah, the 70s!

I head off for the final part of today's journey and for the first time I hear a voice in my head saying 'how much further?' I'm in a bit of pain and unaccountably begin to feel grumpy. To add insult to injury, my hitherto good sense of direction fails, like a satnav that loses connection, and I can't find my hotel. I bumble on for another half hour before finally finding it. To make me even more grumpy, it has no bath, just a shower the size of an upended coffin. As I take my shower I feel a smarting and discover that my left calf is really badly burnt. I am dreading tomorrow – day five – which according to my guidebook is 'very tough indeed', but then catch myself. Surely that's the point of this walk, to challenge myself? It's bad enough that I'm opting for such a soft travel option. I think of Hannah and Victoria and feel more than a little ashamed.

Villafranca del Bierzo is another pretty little town on a river. I go downstairs to sit in the small courtyard of my hotel for a *cerveza*, and sharing my table are three young people, two girls and a boy, probably in their early twenties. We get chatting. They are triplets, American, and they're walking with their parents. I think this is charming. They have been having an erudite conversation which I have crashed into asking if they are writers – they are very chuffed at this. As I go into dinner a bit later the boy, Thomas, comes over to my table and invites me to join them, and despite my rule of not engaging with folk and staying alone, they seem so lovely that I grab the allotted bottle of red wine that comes with my package and plonk it with theirs on their table. I have a really enjoyable evening as the entire family are great fun, and I'm envious of their loving, happy relationship. My childhood was a million miles from this. Marcia and Tom Fulham are mom and dad, they live in Washington DC and she's a hoot. She was a captain in the Navy and he brought the kids up. Her humour is both sharp and quite naughty and appeals to me.

We have a great evening chewing the fat and again I really miss Jimmy. He would have loved to chat with them and they would have loved him. It's such a tragedy that so many people will now never have the opportunity to meet him or to experience his incredible writing talent. Before he died we worked together on a drama about two policemen on their night shift in south-east London; I have resolved to try to get this made but I have no idea if it will happen. At least folk would have one more chance to hear his characters speak. As I head to bed I worry that I'm forgetting what it was actually like to have Jimmy in my life, all the daily mundane and magical stuff that made up our relationship. I'm definitely less grumpy as my head hits the pillow, thanks to the wine and good company. I remember that tomorrow is the dreaded tough one but I'm too tired to worry.

Day 5 - Trek Summary
Villafranca del Bierzo to O Cebreiro

For most pilgrims, this day is very tough indeed and without doubt it is a long climb up to O Cebreiro. However, the scenery is so stunning and a very special feeling of isolation surrounding you as you continue upwards takes the 'pain' away. Arrival in O Cebreiro gives the weary traveller an immense feeling of euphoria.

Average Time: 8¼ hours
Ascent: 1231 metres
Descent: 418 metres
Distance: 29 kilometres

CHAPTER 7

THE CAMINO
LESS TRAVELLED

The dreaded Thursday has finally arrived and this pilgrim's progress is a bit slow today. Despite my lovely evening I awake from a horrid dream. Don't worry, I shan't recount it. There are few things worse than listening to someone else's dreams. That drop in spirit when you hear those words 'I had the weirdest dream last night'. You know there's no escape from the inevitable meandering through the subconscious nonsense as it's regurgitated. Freud may well have described dreams as the royal road to the subconscious but he got paid handsomely to listen to them. And anyhow, didn't he only treat women and, from what I can gather, described them as fixated, hysterical or obsessed – mind you, I've come across a few who do fit that bill … So when you hear these words, the best thing to do is to raise your eyebrows quizzically and encouragingly, put your head to one side in the international body language for 'I'm all ears, do tell me' and then drift into mental screen-save. I use the time for useful stuff like coming up with mental shopping lists. You know when to come out of the screen-save with the cue of a line such as 'weird, huh?' It's all over and you are back in the room. But my horrid dream has set me up in quite a bad mood and it's chilly this morning to boot.

My internal satnav has not re-booted and I can make no sense of the guidebook but then I bump into the lovely Hannah and Victoria who thankfully inform me that there are in fact two routes for half of the journey and one is easier than the other. I let them go off to take the high road and opt myself to take the path of least resistance. I know that the second half of the day will be unavoidably brutal so why add to it? However, there has been a mix up and my directions, it turns out, are for the harder route over the mountains. I decide to really try to slow down and stop overtaking as I don't want to burn out, so instead I decide to get behind someone who looks like they know where they are going and hang in their slip-stream. A likely candidate comes by and she's going at a fair lick so I jump in behind. It's great! A bit like being towed. I don't have to look for the yellow arrows and I stop for coffee when she does and leave when she does. I feel a bit like a stalker or perhaps an undercover private eye. I'm sure she wouldn't mind if she knew; it's the Camino after all.

What I've found in these past few days is that the first hour of the day seems to be the toughest. As my body wakes up I find myself doing a mental body scan, feeling where the muscles ache from the day before, and now I've learned that I need to take time to stretch them out. By an hour in, though, I feel a lot better and my mood is much improved. Endorphins are obviously being released willy nilly but there's another factor that raises my spirits – the cyclists. I've not told you about the peddling *peregrinos* yet, have I? They are nearly all male and seem to be mainly either Spanish or Italian. There must be a sort of Camino beauty contest they win in order to ride the route as they are, without exception, as fit as the proverbial butchers' dogs: tanned, toned and generally gorgeous. They pass you with a hearty '*buen Camino*', even when they are cycling uphill, with a blinding white-toothed smile that melts the worst of moods. They become especially enthusiastic when they are freewheeling down a hill, as they whip past in seconds leaving the greeting hanging on the view of their tight lycra-covered rears disappearing into the distance. Then, later, maybe at lunchtime, you come across them lounging around on the grass outside of cafés, looking so very cool and quite, quite louche as they sip an espresso and suck on a strong cigarette. I have developed quite the soft spot for them.

I have decided to picnic on the walk today. Not for financial reasons, just because I can't face another carb-riddled *bocadillo*. So, I've brought lots of fruit, huge Spanish tomatoes and tinned octopus in tomato sauce. The great thing about this walk is that I feel like a small child reacting and responding only to my basic needs – nothing more. When I'm hungry I eat, when I'm thirsty I drink and if I need the loo, I go. There is no looking at clocks to dictate the shape of the day, just feelings and needs in complete tune with my body. I've also found out that giving in and having faith in the Camino is good. To me the Camino is almost a tangible entity and provides what I need when I need it. For example, twice today I've run out of water walking up the brutal two-hour-long mountain road that offers no shade at the hottest part of the day and twice today I've come across a natural stream running down the hill to fill my bottle with and pour over my boiling head (of course I don't possess a protective hat). The earlier day's chill is a distant memory and the sun is quite unremitting. I'm actually finding the day so invigorating despite the steep incline. I'm back into my overtaking mode and find I love walking uphill, and far from being the most onerous day, this is turning out to be my favourite. The anticipation of reaching the top of the steep, winding road with the promise of glorious views is indeed the food of euphoria.

Having walked up a mule track I hit a concrete path and bear left as directed by my guidebook and ascend into the beautiful O Cebreiro. I've ascended a total of 1,231 metres and am shattered, covered in sweat and dust and very, very happy. Now, I just have to find my hotel and I realise I've no directions. There seems to be a festival on and the tiny mountaintop village is bustling and lively. I wander around for half an hour looking for my sorely needed place of rest but find myself going round in circles among the crowds. Finally I see a group of green-clad local constabulary and two are coming towards me. I get out my hotel voucher and approach them, pointing at the name with a '*donde esta?*' My lack of the language is pitiful but I look at them in an apologetic manner hoping they will feel sorry for the dirty, sweaty object in front of them. They examine it and look quite non-plussed, then one says, in a perfect London accent, 'hang on a minute, we'll check for you'. I'm completely gobsmacked at the surreal juxtaposition of the rough Cockney accent against the panoramic Iberian views. It turns out he was born in Pimlico! I told you, the Camino gives you what you need when you need it. With their help I find the hotel – a modest one star but I have a very jolly twin room and the owners are adorable and so helpful. The views are incredible in the town and I am so relieved to have gotten the toughest day of the walk under my belt. By the way, the guidebook estimated the walk to take eight and a quarter hours today and I did it in seven, so there.

There are stalls selling mainly toot and after a quick once-over of the visitors, I realise it's all very down-to-earth (no, I didn't say 'common'!). It's quite refreshing seeing teen mums in leggings and their men sporting earrings and some impressive mullets. Outside my room, which is in a separate block to the hotel tavern, there is a marquee set up with rows of wooden tables and benches. At the front there are two guys stirring massive vats of octopus boiling in what looks like red wine. It smells delicious and folk are sitting at the tables drinking more red wine from glazed earthen jugs and mopping up the wine sauce with massive chunks of rustic-looking bread. Music is playing loudly, it's some sort of Spanish pop and everyone looks chilled and content. I would have stopped to eat but I've got a dinner organised in the hotel later.

I take my much-needed shower; it seems that baths are now a thing of the past but it's hot and I'm grateful. I then wander into town for an early evening beer before dinner. I ache all over but especially my calves. At least I kept them out of the sun today by wearing sweat pants. Every bone in my feet is sore; they are taking quite a pasting. I read the guidebook for tomorrow and it looks much easier and I'm now under the 200 kilometres to Santiago mark. I figure I've clocked up 130 kilometres already.

There's a German group that seem to be taking the same route as me, staying in the same villages and hotels. They are a mixed bunch but the leader is a formidable older woman who wears her steely grey hair in a tight, austere bun. On the end of her sharp nose sits a pair of black thick-rimmed spectacles. I was delighted when I spotted her smoking a pipe. The overall effect is that of a Weimar Republic sculptress or maybe a student at the Bauhaus. I adore her, she will play herself in the movie. She stands out on the Camino but in a strange way she perfectly fits in.

Joseph Campbell – I mentioned him earlier – talked a lot about 'following your bliss'. It is becoming increasingly clear to me that wants and needs are very different. The obvious song lyrics come to mind: 'you can't always get what you want…', it's very true. I think folk spend so much time tearing around after what they want that they never stop to look at what it is they need in life and are in danger of missing their true destiny. Being on the walk and being so much in tune with my basic bodily needs is having the effect of resonating with my emotional needs and allowing the inner voice to come through clearly. Maybe sometimes you have to have blind faith and just follow rather than try to control situations. Dreams can become reality and I do believe that so many of us are frightened of life and indeed of our own potential and hide behind financial worries and family commitments so that we don't have to admit we were too scared to give life a go. I know that for me my life appears to be a continuum of circuitous routes with no focus on a clear path, or maybe that is the path. I've always followed my feelings with regard to work rather than having a strong plan. My CV reflects this. Having been very unhappy in my early twenties working as a (not very good) secretary in the City of London I always knew I didn't need to do this and, having taken myself off travelling round the world, ended up working in TV and film, which was something I would never have believed possible for someone of my background but my dreams won out. I followed my bliss and I like to think it eventually led me to Jimmy. I really do believe that all limitations are self-imposed. Oops, sorry, I'm starting to sound like a self-help book, I do apologise.

I should point out that I'm contemplating all these higher thoughts while indulging in my latest ritual of lying on the floor with my legs up the wall. I find it really helps after the day's walking. I'm thinking I've an hour till dinner so will just chill and then my phone beeps with a text. It's Hannah. She and Victoria have arrived in town and because of the festival they couldn't get into the *albergue*. I look at the spare single bed in my room and without hesitation offer it to the girls if they are happy to get cosy. Of all the things I'd anticipated on this trip, a slumber party was not one of them. They are delighted with the offer and I decide to treat them to dinner. They dump their stuff and avail themselves of my shower. After many weeks in *albergues* they are ecstatic to have a hot shower with clean, fluffy towels and thrilled at the offer of dinner. They are fabulous company and I love their youth and enthusiasm. We tuck into a gorgeous meal with plenty of chilled wine. I talk about Jimmy and am babbling away while I eat. I look up and discover them both very still with huge, fat tears in their eyes and realise that they are not ready to embrace the type of sadness that has become a normal part of my existence. I pour wine for us all and propose a toast to the Camino and they cheer up. The American family are at the next table and we exchange banter. One of their daughters, Elizabeth, had become sick with heatstroke but two old ladies drove her to O Cebreiro, only accepting two euros on the proviso that they pray for them in Santiago. It just shows how much faith is placed in the power of prayer; in these parts, it's very touching.

After dinner we turn in and, exhausted, drift off to sleep. It's short-lived as an enthusiastic band in town strike up. They play cover versions of songs until 3am when they pull the plug after an awful version of 'The Final Countdown'. As I drift off to sleep I wonder if there's actually a good version.

Day 6 - Trek Summary
O Cebreiro to Triacastela

A stunning day lies ahead of you especially if the weather is fine. It is more than likely you will set off in fog and drizzle but as you descend this usually clears. The Camino at this stage stays high in the Cordillera Cantabrica and hamlets are tiny with few facilities.

Average Time: 7 hours
Ascent: 150 metres
Descent: 570 metres
Distance: 21 kilometres

CHAPTER 8

STUCK IN THE
MIDDLE WITH ME

I'm halfway through the walk and I'm very happy this morning when I wake just before dawn. Hannah and Victoria are sleeping so peacefully I decide to let them carry on as it's still so early. They told me that in the *albergues* people get up as early as 4.30am so they can get on the road and arrive at the next *albergue* to get a bed. I can understand why this is but I'm so glad I don't have to do that as I love starting my walk after a good breakfast, and in the light of day.

Having told you my feelings about other people's dreams, I shall now begin today by telling you about my dream last night. Feel free to go into screen-save mode. It was very vivid and reiterates how powerful the Camino is. It was no Dali-esque odyssey, it was quite the opposite and I was struck when I woke by just how mundane a dream it was. It involved me and Jimmy in our house discussing re-decorating a room and really just hanging out. I'd bought deckchairs that he loved and we talked about his latest writing gig and how we would use the proceeds to finish doing up the house. The dream was marvellous as it felt just like being with him. I'd been so scared to lose that. I'd asked the Camino to not let me forget him and it had delivered with some subconscious film-making. A truly sliding-doors moment, I suppose. It was both beautiful and heart-breaking.

After taking an early morning walk around the village I decide to wake Hannah as the sun is almost up and I suspect there will be a spectacular sunrise that she would want to photograph. She is appreciative and she wakes Victoria. We head out of the hotel room together and having thanked me profusely (which was unnecessary as they made this particular rest place very special) we part company and I head for my much-needed breakfast as once again I'm starving. It is served in the nearby tavern and as I enter I hear a very London accent next to me proclaim, 'John, I have never seen such huge croissants! They must be record breaking!' I chuckle as John's friend is quite correct: on the bar counter is a plate piled high with the most enormous croissants you could imagine. I polish one off with no trouble. The Fulhams arrive and I ask after Elizabeth. It turns out I'm actually talking to her, she and her sister really are identical. Tom looks at the ugly sandals I'm sporting and remarks 'oh, is it sandal day already, it's gone so fast'. I'd told him when we first met of my footwear rotation and it tickles me he's remembered. I tell him that it seems to be doing the job as I've no blisters on my feet; I quickly touch the wooden bar top, just in case.

The walk today is billed as seven hours without a break. Elizabeth and her sister have warned me that downhill can be worse than up, but I love it and complete it in four hours and forty-five minutes. The weather is perfect, sunny but with a good breeze. As I stroll through one village an old lady comes out of her gingerbread-style cottage in the woods bearing a plate stacked with hot pancakes. Of course I'm hungry and I take one gratefully: it tastes like heaven. She is accompanied by a lovely big dog who begrudges me every mouthful of the unexpected treat. I notice the dogs tend to be German Shepherds along the Camino, which to me makes a change from the ubiquitous bundles of muscle I am used to in south-east London. Turns out she's a fixture on the Camino and regularly gives out pancakes to passing pilgrims.

I spend the morning walking through some very pretty, rustic villages and as I turn into one particularly steep stony track up to Alto de San Roque I come across a massive and very dramatic bronze statue of a windswept pilgrim, staff in hand. I sit at his feet for a while and take in the landscape; mountains as far as I can see. My stomach growls so I continue on to the little village of Biduelo for lunch and a stamp in my passport. The latter is getting quite full now and next to my fleece and my sticks is my most treasured possession. I love the variety of the stamps but I do have a particular fondness for the first one that had to be cut and pasted in from Leon. That seems such a long time ago.

The rest of the walk is pleasing and all downhill. I wander past some ancient farm buildings and am, for the most part, alone on my journey, which I like. The farms give way to a tree-lined route, which in turn becomes a stone-flagged lane as I approach Triacalestela. It's a very lovely small village surrounded by the green mountains. The hotel stands alone and is quite imposing. It reminds me of a building in the American Wild West. It's white with grey windows, some with balconies, and I'm delighted to discover that my room has one of them. It's basic but comfortable and really quite large with my bed in the middle of the room. There's also little in the way of sound-proofing as I can hear all the goings on outside my door.

I spy a computer in the reception for guest use and fleetingly wonder if I should check my emails but decide against it. I don't want to thrust myself back into that reality just yet. I do, however, opt to text Jimmy's mum. Jimmy's parents are really lovely people and I know she will worry and I realise I quite like the thought that someone will be worried about me. I let her know how far I've walked and that I'm having a grand time, I'm sure she'll like that. I haven't drunk enough water today and my legs feel slightly swollen. I think it's because there was such a cool breeze that I hadn't felt as thirsty. I need to keep an eye on that. It's a strange feeling being halfway through the trip and having over 150 kilometres under my belt. To have come so far when it wasn't so long ago that a half-hour trip on a bus from my home to the local town seemed an epic and nigh-on impossible journey.

It's only 1pm and as I step out onto my balcony I spy Hannah and Victoria walking past on the street two floors beneath me, and at the same time I receive a text from Hannah saying if I fancy a bowl of *pulpo* and a beer to give her a shout; I'm able to literally do just that. I run out into the sunshine and tag along with my buddies to a lovely small bar in the only street that runs through the village. There are a couple of shops, the ubiquitous *albergues* and that's it.

We have a lovely lazy lunch. Hannah has me in fits of giggles as she recounts adventures of their earlier trip when they were crossing the border from France. Apparently she had horrific blisters and at one *albergue* there was a woman who would visit and pop the blisters then treat them with iodine. This was an agonising experience and had brought her to tears, but the woman had come prepared with her own method of distracting her patients from the pain: a calendar depicting 'hot priests'. Seriously! Hannah had kept the back page from the calendar with the twelve gorgeous men of the cloth shown for each month. We all agree that Monsignor May is the fittest but it's a close-run thing with Father February. It's hilarious. The girls are heading on to Samos, a town ten kilometres further on. If I hadn't been booked in to my hotel I would have joined them as I felt I could easily have walked for another couple of hours. I realise I'm averaging two hours less than the listed guide times despite trying to take more rests along the way and pace myself. I'm just a fast walker and that's that, I guess.

When they leave, Hannah gives me a hug and frets that we might not see one another again on the trip but I say that I'm sure we will. She'd had the great idea of giving people stamped addressed postcards to her home address in Florida so that when she gets home she'll have them to come back to. She gives me one. She's so very sweet and seems to look after Victoria. Given Victoria's looks and figure I can't help thinking that she'll have no worries whatsoever being looked after in life.

My pre-booked dinner that evening turns out to be at the cute bar where I had lunch with the girls. As I sit in the restaurant/bar I wish I had a Kindle as I'm almost finished with the only book I threw in at the last minute – a biography of Hattie Jacques. It's actually very good but I feel I should be reading Lorca or Cervantes while I'm here or maybe something spiritual like Paulo Coelho. But instead I get out my journal and write; it'll give me something to read in a couple of days as I do seem to have the capacity for entertaining myself with my scribblings. The quote by the young Gwendolen Fairfax in *The Importance of Being Earnest* comes to mind: 'I never travel without my diary. One should always have something sensational to read on the train.' It's not an arrogant thing, I don't think, it's more that when I read stuff that I've written back after a period of time it really feels like someone else's words and I wonder where they came from.

When I first started my walk I used to mind eating alone but now I couldn't care less and really quite enjoy it. I have noticed that the dinner time is getting later and is now around 9pm, which isn't great having built up a huge appetite on the walk. I'm content to people-watch and there are so many to pick from. There are two German guys who I first saw at the café in Hospital de Orbigo early on in my journey. They have been following exactly the same route as me and I see them at least three times a day. They are sitting next to one another eating dinner, which I find odd – why wouldn't you sit opposite your dining companion? I don't think they are gay but I can't tell, my 'gaydar' seems switched off on the Camino. I really miss Jimmy. As I've said before, we loved people-watching – it was one of our favourite pastimes, to speculate on and invent their backgrounds. We had a shorthand for summarising personalities using the phrase 'he/she's no stranger to'.

So it could be 'she's no stranger to a Dick Francis novel', or 'he's no stranger to a dark room'. It worked for us. I actually think a big part of the attraction of taking this trip was the fact that there was no way that Jimmy could have done this. I know that hiking two hours up a sun-drenched mountain path would in no way lead me to miss his company; he could never have done it, not with his poorly heart. But sitting in a mountain village restaurant, drinking a glass of the chilled local wine in the perfect warmth of the evening sun, coming up with back-stories for the other diners, I miss him. He'd have loved it – especially the wine.

I've ordered a mixed salad to start but I am getting sick of them; I think it's the tinned tuna. As the waiter puts it in front of me I wonder what to do as I really have no appetite for it. The problem is solved with the arrival of a late diner, a striking black and ginger cat. I catch his eye as I surreptitiously put down a piece of fish. He's clearly over the moon (I'm assuming it's a 'he' – aren't all ginger cats?) although being a cat would never admit it, and adopts the 'I could take it or leave it but I chose to take it this time to help you out' attitude. I fall in love with him. He sticks around and proves to be an amiable companion as he polishes off the first course and waits patiently for the next, cleaning himself politely in between. I've ordered a fat steak and he relieves me of the fat from it and, eating this, he tolerates a couple of minutes of me tickling him under the ear before excusing himself. A group of French diners have arrived and, having spotted the beautiful creature, continue to offer him a further course. He's doing very well tonight.

A lovely old man who looks like an older Patrick Stewart and must be pushing his late 70s approaches my table. He asks where I'm from and I tell him London. He laughs and says he speaks no English but manages to get across that he'd seen me alone and thought he should come and join me. I thank him but gently make it clear that I'm fine. He points to my journal that I'd been writing in between the cat feeding and says 'you scribe a book?' I think about it and then nod, yes, I am indeed. He leaves me to my scribing as I wait for coffee and another elderly gent approaches – what's this all about? He's very sweet and is the spitting image of the old man in the movie *Up*. He is another German and chats to me in the language for quite a while before I have to confess I am English. He had assumed I was German. I'm guessing it's the blonde hair, or the hearty calves. I explain that my secondary school German lessons have only left me with a couple of phrases, one being 'are you sick I'm so sorry to hear that' and the other 'my dog's called Lumpy'. He laughs as I recite both in German and then heads back to his table.

Patrick Stewart returns. With broken English he asks if he can take his after dinner coffee with me. I don't mind and it transpires that he is in fact from Belgium. That's a game changer as I can hold my own in French, so we're off chatting. Before you know it I've managed to confidently let him know '*mon mari est mort*' (at least I know this is correct whereas I've been fretting since Leon that the miming of my fingers across my throat to the taxi driver and hotel receptionist might have indicated that I'd murdered my husband). He pats my hand sympathetically then tells me that he's walked the Camino fourteen times. I wonder why. He has three children and three grandchildren but his wife has no problem with him going off to be the happy wanderer. I wonder if she does some wandering of her own while he's away. He asks me if I could excuse him for a minute and bizarrely leaves me and his coffee and heads out of the restaurant. About ten minutes later he returns with a very pretty posy of wild flowers tied with a bow that he ceremoniously presents to me. It's very touching and I thank him and later, in my room, I put them in a small plastic water bottle by my bed. When he leaves the waiter tells me that he is known as the '*Homme de fleurs*'.

He heads off to his *albergue* and I say goodbye to the well-fed cat and go back to my room. It's only 9.30pm but I'm shattered. I put on the TV, something I've avoided doing as it feels as if it goes against the Camino vibe. But I rationalise that it's ok if I can't understand what's being said and anyway before long I'm turning off both the TV and the light. A couple of hours later, in semi-slumber, I wonder why the people sharing my room are being so noisy and as I wake fully I realise that I'm alone and the noise is coming from the room upstairs (I told you the sound-proofing was inadequate). They are very enthusiastic and their bed is very creaky. I dig out my earplugs and go back to sleep. Another hour goes by and I'm awoken once more but this time with an almighty thirst. I reach out in the dark for my water bottle and taking a huge swig find myself almost choking on a mouthful of wild flowers. Bloody *homme de fleurs*.

Day 7 - Trek Summary
Triacastela to Sarria via San Xil

With fine weather the most beautiful day lies ahead. Apart from the early up hills the rest is gentle downwards to Sarria. Take care over the last 4 kilometres as the path offers no shade and can be very hot.

Average Time: 6 hours
Ascent: 300 metres
Descent: 460 metres
Distance: 18 kilometres

CHAPTER 9

A RIVER RUNS THROUGH IT

Today starts out as one of my favourite days so far. As much as I've loved walking through mountains punctuated by small hamlets, I now find myself in what appears to be endless woods and the shade is extremely welcome. The route my guidebook suggests is via San Xil but I choose the alternative route and it turns out to be the best choice as after two and a half hours walking I hit the gorgeous town of Samos. It's staggeringly beautiful and the monastery is a Unesco World Heritage Site. I stop to take a photo and an English girl comes up to me asking if I would take her photo with the monastery in the background. 'You're fast,' she says as she heads off. So, I'm getting a Camino reputation, am I? I decide to look around the monastery and as I enter I encounter the German *Up* man coming out. 'You need fruit and nuts,' he declares as he thrusts a packet towards me. I'm not sure if he's asking me or telling me but I hold out my hand anyhow and receive a pile of healthy treats. I thank him and he beams back.

The monastery is bordered by a beautiful river called the Oribio. I say it out loud as it's a pleasing shape and sound. I try saying it while trilling the 'r' and it resembles a cheer. I want to throw up one hand and snap my fingers while stamping one foot but I'm aware that I'm already looking quite daft standing on an ancient bridge talking to myself. The river adds its own musical accompaniment to the setting as it bubbles underneath. I walk further around the town and come across another lovely bridge; this one has fourteen iron scallop shells along it. I stand looking down at the river and a young man approaches and out of the blue informs me that it is rich in trout and eels. So, it would have suited both Jimmy and me, him fishing the trout and me eating the eels. It's quite cloudy and as usual I'm ahead of myself with today's walk so instead of a café lunch I decide to treat myself to a hearty lunch in a lovely restaurant opposite the monastery. At first I wonder what reception I'll get given my walking attire but it's practically empty and the couple of other diners look like pilgrims too so I soon feel at home. I feast on Galician soup, scallops in their shells and round it all off with a slice of the delicious *torta Santiago* – a dense almond cake spiked with the zest of oranges and lemons. The tables have cloths on them and I feel quite decadent; it was a very good choice although I feel like a nap after all that food. I collect my stamp as I pay the bill. It isn't expensive by London standards but certainly more than I've been used to along the route, but I feel I deserve it.

The walk from Samos is a bit boring and I charge on ahead at full steam. If I've got a reputation for speed I may as well live up to it. I'm glad I've a full stomach as yesterday I made the huge mistake of letting myself run out of gas. All these hours of walking is like running a car, you have to make sure you have the fuel for the journey. If my body were a car it would just be a 'run around', lots of short trips with the petrol lasting a long time. However, now I'm on the walking equivalent of a Grand Prix and if fuel and water aren't kept up in pit stops then I realise that I will stop. Just like that. I was about to embark on climbing yet another hill yesterday and I realised I couldn't, I would have to eat something first. It was a really strange feeling as I had to sit down where I was and eat some fruit and drink water before I could put another foot forward. Today's late lunch ensures that this will not happen for the rest of the day.

Later on in the day I start getting a twinge in my right knee, which develops into an unremitting pain. It's so bad that for the first time on the walk I feel quite helpless. Elizabeth's warning a few days earlier about going downhill being worse is now a reality for me. I wonder if it will hurt less if I walk backwards, and discover that it does in fact help a bit. It seems that the only way to go forward is to go backwards. I'm no longer the fastest on the Camino and I start to worry that I won't be able to finish if this injury is going to be long lived. I sit down on a rock in the middle of the woodlands and have a good cry. It's the first I've had since Leon and I feel so wretched and so far from anyone I love or who loves me and I'm in pain. Why did I think I could do this? I'm sure that I'll have to stop now and give up.

In the midst of this desperation I think of my lovely bereavement counsellor, Sue, and what she'd have to say about this state of affairs. I know she would be encouraging me onwards and be proud of what I've achieved so far considering the mess she found me in this January. It had all started with my obsession with a bereavement forum I'd found when I'd Googled 'grief'. I devoured all the biographies of the members and added my own tale of woe. At first it was a huge comfort and I lost many hours to it, although, I hate to admit it, but being me I started to judge people and allot them a pecking order in terms of whether their grief was more or less painful than mine. For example, one poor woman was distraught about losing an elderly parent so I put her below me because I figured a) he was elderly and b) he was her father and surely that's the natural order. I then came upon a woman who was definitely above me and who had written very eloquently and openly about the hell she was living since her husband died and left her in a strange country (England) with in-laws who despised her and no money, so she won that round of bereavement Top Trumps.

After a couple of weeks I could see this was becoming unhealthy, and after reading about one woman who was in just as much pain three years after her loss I quit. I know I'll still miss Jimmy in three years, in ten years, I'll always miss him, but the thought of still being in that much pain was awful. I Googled 'grief' again and this time found a bereavement counselling charity in my neighbourhood who were willing to send someone to my house once a week for six months for a very low fee. It became my lifeline and a safe place to sit and be with Jimmy – friends and family can only take so much of your pain. She was gentle but firm with me and suggested that perhaps I might actually go and cash in the prescription for antidepressants I'd been given after the overdose. It had sat in my purse for a couple of weeks. Maybe it was pride or shame in admitting I needed medicinal help that had stopped me actually getting them. Sue pointed out that I had a very valid reason to be feeling so awful and likened it to refusing an anaesthetic while having a limb amputated. She had a point so I did as she suggested and it did help me to start to move out of the pitch blackness towards some sort of light.

So thinking of Sue, I manage to calm myself down and sit for a while, just being. No one passes me and it's very quiet. I have no idea how long I stay there in a sort of meditative state but eventually I snap out of it and manage to hobble up and not for the first time am thankful for my sticks. I stumble into Sarria and find my hotel. It's quite fancy schmanzy and I instantly cheer up; that's how shallow I can be. I spot the Americans. I've still beaten them in terms of time as I've showered and am sitting outside the hotel with a beer when they arrive dishevelled from the day's walk. I think they spend much more time smelling the roses than I do and I guess that with five of them it just makes the going a little slower. I head off to find a pharmacy and purchase a bandage for my knee; as soon as I put it on I feel better and am instantly cheered and feel more confident about being able to complete the walk. The range of emotions I can go through in one day is quite exhausting.

The town is small but still feels quite urban compared to the other places I've stayed and my hotel is by a dusty rail track. It reminds me of a setting for an early twentieth-century American novel, something penned by Edith Wharton perhaps or F. Scott Fitzgerald. I remember that I have to come back here by cab after I walk as hotels in Portomarin were fully booked when the travel company arranged my itinerary but that's fine; going backwards seems to be a theme today. Feeling inspired by the lovely hotel and my bandaged knee I become quite practical before dinner and wash out some underwear and put it on the windowsill to dry. Later I hook up with the Fulhams in the restaurant and, feeling quite proud of my domesticity, tell them about my laundry ventures. They look at me and laugh; they have each literally packed all their belongings in a small backpack and wash out their clothes every evening as they only have two sets of t-shirts and shorts! I go to bed and gather up my clean, dry knickers from the windowsill – I'm still proud of myself! I take off my knee bandage, hop into bed and pray that my knee will be ok tomorrow as it's supposed to be a 'stiff morning climb'.

Just before I go to sleep I turn on my phone and there's a lovely text from Jimmy's mum. As I suspected, she's grateful for me letting her know that I'm safe. It's lovely to feel connected so I decide to do something I said I wouldn't do on the walk and send out a group text to some friends in the UK. After my wee breakdown in the woods earlier I want to reach out and connect, it just feels like a good thing to do and I instantly feel less lonely.

Day 8 - Trek Summary
Sarria to Portomarin

After a fairly stiff morning climb, most of the day ambles down through lanes covering a total distance of 21 kilometres to Portomarin.

Average Time: 7 hours
Ascent: 240 metres
Descent: 340 metres
Distance: 21 kilometres

CHAPTER 10

CLAIRE'S KNEE

I wake up much later this morning and lie in bed with my thoughts till gone 9am, and even though the weather is grey, my knee feels ok when I get up and tentatively test it, which is a relief and encourages me. I pack the bandage anyhow and grab a quick breakfast before heading out at 9.30am.

As I leave the town I'm behind two German boys and one starts talking to me in his native language. I respond in English and he tells me it's his first day's walk and asks me if it was mine. I proudly tell him I've been walking now for eight days and might just as well have added 'hah, bloody amateurs' and realise I've become a Camino snob. The road is packed with walkers. They all seem squeaky clean and fresh and for some reason a lot of the women are made-up and wearing dangly earrings – did I miss the memo?

Then two hours into the walk I start to descend a steep hill and halfway down my knee goes and it's agony. I hobble to the bottom and fortunately there's an *albergue* to get coffee and a *sello* and put on the bandage, not that it seems to make much difference. The descent today is 340 metres so pretty much the rest of the day from here on in. I experiment with different ways of going down. I find I can trot uphill like a mountain goat but any whiff of a descent and there's immediate dissent from my knee. It's so upsetting but I persevere. The scenery is mainly farms with accompanying strong farm smells. It's like walking through a Spanish version of *The Archers*. It also feels more commercial and, despite my injury, I will still arrive early in Portomarin.

When I next stop for a coffee I turn on my phone and it explodes like a 'howler' in Harry Potter with messages in response to my missive last night. It is lovely to be reading so many encouraging responses and gives me a much-needed boost. I then realise that by having to go back to Sarria to stay at the same hotel again tonight I won't see any recognisable faces as I'll be out of sync and this dulls my mood. I know I'm being a baby about it but I don't want to go back to what seems a big town, I want the intimacy of a small village and the comfort of familiar faces. In Sarria it will be the next shift arriving. I catch myself moaning – enough, Claire! Get on with it!

I continue to go down backwards. I'm not in so much pain but I feel very stupid. One other, slightly more dignified method is to walk with my left foot at right angles to my right foot (I did say it was only slightly more dignified) and leaning heavily on the sticks (how I love those sticks). My friend's little girl has been known to underline any pain by stressing 'but it reeeeeallllllly hurts' and I find myself echoing this in my head. I'm worrying how I'll get through the final few days. I will now pay close attention to the descents on each day and as far as I can remember they outnumber the ascents. I guess I've been lucky so far and my hubris at being able to do the walk with no training has come back to bite me firmly on my ample behind.

It's 3pm and in order to get to Portomarin I am faced with crossing the longest, highest bridge over a river that I have ever walked on. I've never shirked from a bit of daredevil behaviour involving heights; I've always headed to the highest slide in water parks. When I bungee-jumped in New Zealand my only reservation was the fact that my weight would be written on my hand for all to see. I had no qualms about throwing myself off a disused railway bridge with only elastic round my ankles. When Jimmy and I lived in Manchester working on a TV show he was writing, he drove me to Blackpool one day solely to ride the biggest rollercoaster in Europe, aptly named 'The Big One'. Obviously it was out of bounds for him with his poorly heart but he enjoyed sharing my childlike delight when faced with a bunch of twisted metal configured to induce terror. He held my bag while I happily ran off to join the mainly male, mainly teenaged thrill-seekers heading for the entrance. I was wearing a bright orange cardigan and he loved recounting afterwards how he looked up following the car I was in as it took the most nosebleed-inducing drop. According to him, the other riders were gripping the bar in front of them with grim faces but in the middle there was a pair of orange arms stuck defiantly up in the air.

So it's quite a shock to me that just a few steps onto the bridge I find myself feeling dizzy and a little nauseous. When did I develop vertigo? Here I am experiencing fear that develops into terror with every step. Where did that daredevil go? Is this part of grief too or just getting older? I figure that the best course of action is to walk as fast as I can and get it over with but I'm behind an elderly guy who is walking at a torturously slow pace and I can't overtake him and he seems quite untroubled by the height. We finally make it to the other side and the last hurdle to get into the town is a huge flight of stone steps that do my knee no favours but at least are uphill.

When I finally get into the town square of Portomarin I'm surprised that despite all my ailments I've undercut the stated time by two and half hours. I have the number for the taxi that will take me back to Sarria and they seem to have been expecting my call. While I wait for their arrival

outside a café I chat to an English girl. She's rolling a cigarette and tells me she's been walking for three weeks and that
she's noticed me along the way and how fast I'm walking.
She then adds 'We thought you must be German' – ah, so
is that it? Is it my speed that gives me a Teutonic air? Maybe
that's why the lad at the beginning of today's walk spoke to
me in German. The taxi arrives swiftly to deposit me back in
Sarria. It's only 3pm and dinner isn't till 9pm so I re-pack my
bag and charge my phone and camera battery before taking a
bath and deciding to see if I can find the Old Town of Sarria
and maybe even something that's open.

It's actually quite chilly as I wander around. I don't have
a map but have this notion that I'll find what I'm looking
for if I head to the main church, and just as this thought
forms I hear church bells ringing out. The main road soon
gives way to a steep hill, which is home to a very cute group
of cobbled streets overlooking the hills. It's a lovely spot
but I find myself really missing Jimmy. As I said earlier, I've
had quite lengthy periods of my life living alone without a
partner. And it's been fine. I have friends whose relationships
have overlapped and have effectively never really been alone
in their adult life, which is obviously fine too. So theoretic-
ally I should be able to just go back to that way of living.
If only it were that easy. The clichéd line of 'better to have
loved and lost…' rings as strongly as the church bells but it

makes me angry. I can't just revert back to that person. I'm not that person anymore. I can't even walk over a bridge and today's experience feels like a huge metaphor for where I am post-Jimmy. Scared and alone. I realise I've sat on a bench by the church for some time now and I'm crying again. I don't want to be alone, or more accurately I don't want to not be with Jimmy. It is so hugely unfair. It really isn't better to have loved and lost, believe me. But would I rather have never had him in my life? If I'd have been told I only had that set period with him would I have embarked on the relationship in the first place? Yes, of course I would. Our relationship showed me what it is to truly love a person and trust them implicitly with your heart and soul. I remember reading the line from the Prophet about love, describing the 'pillars of the temple' standing apart but being supportive, which is how we were. Jimmy had no problem if I wanted to go hiking with a friend in Cuba or take a few days to visit a pal in Switzerland. He didn't really like flying but was happy for me to do my own thing.

Most of the time, though, I loved just hanging out with him at home, cooking and listening to Radio Four in the evenings. If we were both working at home but in different rooms he'd send me emails addressed to 'Miss Russell on the first floor' in which he'd create a character of a love-struck subordinate humbly contacting the object of his affection.

I still have those exchanges. They're very funny, but I can't bring myself to read such a vivid example of the simplicity of our love and the daily fun and comfort we took in each other's company. Not yet. Maybe one day I'll be able to revisit them but right now the very memory brings more tears coursing down my sunburnt cheeks.

I head back to my hotel, eat dinner and decide to have an early night. I'm actually looking forward to tomorrow and getting back in sync with the Camino, seeing the familiar faces. I will be given a lift to Portomarin in the morning and I can't believe there are only three days' walking till Santiago. All the crying today has actually been cathartic and I feel incredibly calm tonight.

Day 9 - Trek Summary
Portomarin to Palas del Rei

A longer day of 25 kilometres with most of the route following the road; however, traffic is light and the afternoon is especially tranquil with the advantage that you can maintain a steady pace.

Average Time: 8 hours
Ascent: 240 metres
Descent: 450 metres
Distance: 25 kilometres

CHAPTER 11

THE LUCK OF THE IRISH

It's Monday today and, unlike Sir Bob's song, I find that I do like them. The bad mood yesterday has dissolved and I wake feeling quite cheery and looking forward to today's walk. For a start the descent is considerably shorter than the ascent so that's a huge bonus, although my knee is feeling a lot better but I don't want to tempt fate. I'm glad to be out of the Groundhog Day of having to spend two nights in Sarria. Soon the entire sky is a beautiful blue and after breakfast I travel back to Portomarin with the luggage. The woman driving the small van has insured herself with a vast array of religious icons hanging from her rear-view mirror and on the dashboard. I feel more than a little protected on our journey. I glance back at all the rucksacks and cases and instantly see mine and it makes me smile. I'm dropped off at the foot of a steep hill but that's cool. Up is good. I've taken no chances despite my knee feeling ok and have put the support bandage on and necked two ibuprofen, the walker's equivalent of religious icons, I guess.

It was odd being in the hotel last night and I felt out of kilter with the guests staying there. I suppose it's because so far I've been used to the sense of forward propulsion, of gaining on the kilometres daily. Also it seemed as though my fellow guests were mostly French, not that that's a bad thing, it's just that for once I actually felt like talking to people but was too tired to battle through language barriers. I like being back on track although there are so many folk on the walk today despite my guide saying 'traffic is lighter'. I can't feel the Camino so much as the airwaves feel jammed. There are a lot of groups of Irish folk too, for some reason, and the cafés are all packed. I had planned to stop for a coffee at around eleven this morning at a café mentioned in my guide book but when I arrive, despite being in the middle of woodlands, the outside seating looks more like a motorway café with one guy downing a bottle of beer while barking into his mobile phone. I feel nostalgic for my days in Rabinal, Monlinaseca and O Cebreiro. There was an innocence and a ruggedness that was charming compared to today, which feels more like being in Piccadilly Circus.

I stop for lunch and recognise 'John's mate' (he of the big croissants observation) from O Cebreiro. We exchange mutterings about how the vibe has changed so much. The garden area is busy but I find a spot under a tree and wait for my mixed salad. I spotted two very cute cats when I came in and their location influenced my seating choice as I know I can shamelessly gain the affection of my feline friends with tuna. One is obviously part Siamese with pale blue eyes. As with most Siamese cats she is very chatty. The other is grey and white and likes a tickle on her tummy. A family consisting of a dad and three teenagers sit at a table near to me. I'm not sure what nationality they are but obviously not from an animal-loving nation. The cats approach enthusiastically and are quite viciously rebuked. I notice the stodgy food they are eating and think to myself that certainly one of the teenagers wouldn't have hurt giving up some of her food to the cats given the size of her thighs. I wish them blisters and pulled tendons and throw in sore knees for good measure.

After lunch I head off and manage to find a quieter stretch through woods. I get a little lost as there are quite a few twists and turns so I have to be alert in order to spot the yellow arrows. I've found that I've been able previously to pick them up without really thinking about them, it really is like programming a satnav. The subconscious just gets used to 'seeing' them, but now I have to really focus to find them and it's quite tiring. I come across a stream and realise I have to cross it via some precariously placed stones. Safely across I allow myself a little sit down in the peace of the woods. I try to de-clutter my brain and attempt to meditate but the excitement I'm feeling about imminently completing my walk means I'm unable to really be still so I get up and carry on to Palas de Rei.

My pension is modest but perfectly adequate. I don't see any of the usual suspects but there are a group of around eight lively Irish women who I get chatting to at the bar. They invite me to join them for dinner and I happily accept. They are very funny and I find myself partaking of much more of the chilled red than I have in the past. God bless the Irish! I think the fact that I'm quite giddy at the thought of finishing my walk and of my knee not hurting has added to my euphoria. I talk to them about Jimmy and of course have to let them know my grandmother was Irish.

Seeing as I'm among a group of obviously good friends and I have got my chatty head on I decide to also tell them about my friend Lizzie from Los Angeles. She'd been a bridesmaid at my first wedding in 1993 but somehow we'd lost touch after I moved back to London and it was only when I walked past a movie poster outside a cinema while working in Glasgow several years later that I saw her name listed as the screenwriter. I was so proud that she'd achieved what she'd always wanted to and was obviously now a successful screenwriter with a Hollywood film to her name. I managed to track her down through her agent and start up an email conversation and it was like we'd never lost touch. She's the most grounded person I know – caring and very, very funny.

The previous year Jimmy and I had been out to LA to visit her and of course they were best friends in minutes being of the same writers tribe. For me, it was like having a sister back.

I'd emailed her a couple of weeks before Jimmy died to see if she could come over for a Christmas party I was planning, but she was too busy with work. Cut to three days after he died and there was lovely Lizzie, wheeling her suitcase up my snow-covered front path. All she'd asked for was my address and had gotten onto three flights to be with me. I couldn't believe it, it was such a gift and I can't begin to express how much her presence meant to all of us. I had someone to 'chum me along', as Jimmy would say, to all those horrible but unavoidable appointments like visiting the funeral home and registering the death. She even helped me put together the order of service, which suddenly became incredibly important to me; I had to get it right and the Christmas holidays looming made deadlines tight. I left her one day to her own devices, asking her to see if she could source a printing company who could get the booklets produced on time. To be honest, I really didn't hold out much hope of a girl from Hollywood finding someone to help us in south-east London at such short notice, but by the time I got home not only had she found someone, but the guy lived in my neighbourhood and would come over to pick up photos, etc that very afternoon. It was incredible.

In some bizarre way those days between the death and the funeral were at times, dare I say it, enjoyable. I know that sounds bonkers but the house was full of people and we were constantly cobbling meals together in the evening for anything up to twelve people. It kept Jimmy alive and felt so comforting with my lovely Lizzie at the heart of it. She met my friends and Jimmy's family and charmed all who met her. She stayed until Christmas Eve and I could not be more grateful for her help given with such love and grace. Lizzie is an Angelino through and through and hates the cold as much as Jimmy did, but there she was in one of the worst winters in decades, trudging through the snow with me all over south-east London, being there when I needed to cry (a lot) or laugh (quite a lot too), and then would melt away when I needed to be alone. My new best Irish friends agree that Lizzie is indeed a mensch (I think I'm the one to use that word). The Irish ladies find the story really moving and I worry that I've brought down the mood but they enthusiastically order more wine and take over the conversation telling me stories of their own for another hour or so.

As I lie in bed, slightly squiffy, I read my itinerary for the remaining days and am reminded that the penultimate day's walk gets me to Lavacolla and the last day is then only a ten-kilometre walk to Santiago, which is a mere stroll for me.

I ponder this and for some reason it doesn't sit well. What it means is that I will arrive in Santiago refreshed after such a short walk and I realise that I've somehow envisaged my arrival there involving me being exhausted and almost on my hands and knees at the end of the journey – all much more dramatic. I'm toying with the idea now that I'll just keep going once I hit Lavacolla, and after reaching Santiago and getting my certificate I can get a taxi back to the hotel. This then means I can ride with the luggage to Santiago on the final day and attend my 'Graduation' at the mass refreshed. This idea solidifies into a firm plan of action and it improves my mood even further. I love taking control of a situation, especially if it involves drama.

Day 10 - Trek Summary
Palas del Rei to Arzua via Melide

This is the longest day of the week at close on 30 kilometres and is probably the toughest, but you will feel well rewarded if completing the whole day. It ambles along up and down through some attractive countryside even though the main road is often close by. Set off early and take plenty of short rests.

Average Time: 8.5 hours
Ascent: 200 metres
Descent: 380 metres
Distance: 29 kilometres

CHAPTER 12

PULPO AND PULPITS

I awake with a slight red-wine hangover and know I've been in Irish company! When I go to breakfast the bar area is still dark (it's only 7.30am) but folk are drinking from sherry glasses full of a thick dark syrupy-looking liquor topped off with some sort of clear alcohol – it seems to be doing the trick. I toy with the hair-of-the-dog idea but opt instead for the coffee and croissants also on offer, and feel like getting on the road earlier today so head straight out. I see friend-of-John (John himself doesn't talk), who asks if I'm going to Melide. I proudly tell him that I'm actually going further, to Arzua, and walking the best part of 30 kilometres today. He points out that there is a famous restaurant serving almost exclusively octopus in Melide and I seem to remember reading about it in my guide so thank him for the reminder and make a mental note to stop there.

The road is packed and very noisy with so many folks on mobile phones. I try to pass at least twelve large backpacks with legs sticking out from under them that are directly in front of me but it feels like an impenetrable wall and I have to just hang back behind them for about ten minutes until I find a gap and dart through. I walk alone for another twenty minutes before coming up behind what turns out to be four Irish women, who are obviously on intimate terms with the Blarney Stone. It seems as if they are all talking at once, no one listening to the others and seemingly no breath being taken during the constant cacophony. It's quite entertaining. I leave them behind and get a text from Hannah re the postcard and having a beer when I get to my last hotel. I send back that I'll send the postcard from Santiago, not long now.

I get into Melide at 11am and debate whether to go to the restaurant or not as it's feels too early to get *pulpo*, but as ever I'm hungry despite the time of day and the route takes me right by it so that makes up my mind. The *Pulperia Ezequiel* is obviously a legend on the Camino and is incredibly welcoming with its benches flanking long wooden tables laid out in rows for communal dining. Red and white wine is served in small terracotta bowls to wash down the spicy, salty octopus with hunks of rustic bread. The *pulpo* is boiling in huge vats on massive stoves as I enter and as it's quite early for lunch I have no trouble getting a seat. There's sawdust on the floor and there's no grappling to translate a Spanish menu as the choice is as simple as the decor. I am so very happy I bothered.

I get back on the road at about the same time that folk are stopping for their lunch. The town of Melide dissolves and becomes a beautiful forest and I feel I'm connected back into the Camino. I walk more or less alone and come to a small river, which has to be crossed by stepping on a series of stones. There is a woman wading in the water and a guy sat on the riverbank as I gingerly navigate the makeshift bridge. No one says a word and it's quite magical with the dappled light bouncing off the water. I come to a small empty church and the pulpit, though simple, strikes me as very beautiful. It's empty when I walk in and I suddenly have an urge to go and stand behind the lectern but end up feeling a bit silly so I help myself to a *sello* and I'm off alone again for an hour before coming to yet another church, even smaller than the one before, and again I admire the intricately carved wooden pulpit. This one has a priest who heartily shakes my hand in a grip that is quite a shock to the system. I hope he's a little more gentle when christening babies. He then blesses me and gives me a small piece of card which has on one side a picture of St James and on the other a prayer. As I come out into the sunlight there's Marcia, Tom and the family. It's lovely to see them as it's been days since we've hung out. I tell them that I've just been blessed and Marcia raises an eyebrow saying

'Well I wonder what that will do?' I'm going to miss Marcia. I discuss how the Camino has changed and has such a different feel. Elizabeth tells me that the final 100 kilometres is the minimum amount you can walk and still receive a certificate and that many young people do it to put on their CVs. One hundred kilometres is the distance from Sarria to Santiago so that's why it's so crowded. She shows she's inherited her mother's wit when she says 'It's the delinquents' Camino'.

I anticipate a struggle up to Arzua as described in my guidebook but it's actually not that bad. I decide to stop for a coffee just outside the town and find myself chatting to yet more Irish women, this time a mother and daughter walking the Camino. I'm certainly making up for my days of silence earlier in the walk and I may well have vicariously kissed the Blarney Stone as I can't shut up and spend a couple of hours with them. This works out well as it means I arrive later to my hotel. It's actually the first one I come across and is fine although trying to be a bit boutique and has no bath, but dinner is thankfully early at 7.30pm as I'm starving – I'll take that as a blessing, thank you, Father.

Day 11/12 - Trek Summary
Arzua to Santigo

An easier day of about 29 kilometres lies ahead with the comforting fact that it is mostly downhill from now on to Santiago. Much of the route will follow the main road but still there are many quiet stretches away from the road as you pass through forests and numerous hamlets. Look out for some lovely 'horreos'.

Average Time: 8.5 + 2 hours
Ascent: 200 + 50 metres
Descent: 380 + 90 metres
Distance: 29 + 10 kilometres

CHAPTER 13

SANTIAGO OR BUST

I can't believe it's only eleven days since I started out on the Camino. I get up extra early for my final day's walk and realise I've a whopping 39 kilometres to achieve today in order to get all the way to Santiago. The boots are on rotation, so are the denim shorts as the sunburn has turned into a strip of brown down either calf. I'm not particularly hungry so I just grab a coffee and head out as I want to get going earlier than usual. It's quite busy on the road but as I overtake folk for the last time it thins out and soon I'm in woodlands alone. I feel the urge to stop and sit down and so that's just what I do. I'll miss this sense of following my urges and listening to my body; I can't just sit down in the middle of Lewisham High Street. Well – I could, I guess, but it's probably not wise. I just sit there and look at the trees and realise there are large tears dripping from my chin onto my bare knees. I hadn't even realised I was crying but it feels quite nice and I don't question it, just let the tears fall until I get an urge to be upright once more and forge on westward. Is this how grief will be then? Will I find myself sitting down and crying, then getting up and carrying on for years to come? Forever? The thought doesn't terrify me and I know that the only way to find this out is to just keep going, ever westward towards the setting sun. Sometimes I catch myself making statements like this. I have to remember not to take myself too seriously.

My stomach is complaining that I skipped my croissant but I don't find a café for another hour and a half when I reach a small village. Two very funny Irish women join me for lunch and I tell them I'm writing a daily journal, which fascinates them. I say I'm not sure if I'll put it out there for all to see or whether it's just for me but they are insistent that I should publish it at some stage. We laugh a lot sat outside on a small terrace in the sunshine and it's such a contrast to how I was less than two hours earlier. I stay much longer than I intended as I'm having so much fun but I know I need to get on the road if I want to reach Santiago today. I'm put in mind of the Robert Frost lines 'But I have promises to keep, and miles to go before I sleep'.

I pass by some metal fencing and realise it's a small airport. To confirm this, a small plane flies overhead and I realise its livery is that of the airline I have to engage with once more the day after tomorrow. I make a mental note to look at my packing and make sure I don't get charged for excess baggage again. I can almost feel the frustration of the passengers on the plane who have no doubt been fleeced for various transgressions.

I'm hot and sweaty when I arrive at Lavacolla and almost immediately I spy my pension with its two stars winking at me with the dual promise of a hot shower and a cold beer. It's 4.30pm and my feet are howling for me to stop and I'm tempted for a moment to throw in the towel for today; I've done 29 kilometres after all. But the stubborn streak kicks in and I turn my back on the yellow stars and look instead for the yellow arrows pointing me to my final destination. I hadn't read the itinerary and wasn't prepared for an uphill slog. So I was quite grateful when halfway up the steep road a (gorgeous) Italian cyclist asks me to stop and take his photo. It's quite a fancy camera and he's quite a fussy model so it takes a while but we get there and his fit, lycra-clad image is immortalised. When he's gone I duck into the woods for my last ablution on the Camino before entering Santiago. I'll have to remember not to do that in Lewisham High Street!

The walk is quite ugly as I cross the busy A9 via a bridge and for some strange reason I can't find any signs to the cathedral and seem to be going round in circles. I sit on a bench exhausted, frustrated and about to give up when I hear the sound of bagpipes. It's bizarre and completely unexpected. I follow the surreal wailing to find a be-kilted piper standing under an old stone archway blowing for all he's worth and as I look behind him I see the cathedral. It's like Jimmy has just given me a cultural hand on the last leg. The cathedral is massive and utterly splendid and to add to the drama a solitary pilgrim walks into the Plaza de Camino, one hand holding his huge wooden staff and the other a rope attached to a donkey. It's all just perfect and I feel full of energy as I find the *Officina del Pelegrino* as instructed in my guide-book. I head to the second floor, where I am told that 'the staff are very friendly'. Apparently it's usually mobbed with pilgrims but because it's now 6.30pm it's almost empty. The staff, however, or at least the young woman I encounter, turn out to be far from friendly and I'm reminded of the woman at the airline desk all that time ago in Stansted when I left to come here. Maybe she used to work for them? I hand over my well-worn passport full of the requisite number of daily *sellos* with trepidation. However, she completely redeems herself by preparing the certificate with my name written in what seems to be the Latin equivalent. Instead of Claire Liza Russell I've been immortalised as Clarum Elisabetham Russell – it's very grand; perhaps I should adopt it as my *nom de plume*.

I'm elated as she rolls up the certificate, first checking the ink is dry, and puts it into a cardboard tube for safe carriage home. Home. This time in two days I'll be home, 'Whatever that is' (said in a Blanche Dubois accent). A day or so after the funeral I lost my mobile phone and dialled it from my landline; when I tracked it down the window displayed the word 'Home' and it struck me that my house no longer felt like home without Jimmy in it. It had taken on a very different character and would never feel the same again. I'd bought it and renovated it with Jimmy and we were supposed to live there together. I realise I'm becoming maudlin and I push these thoughts aside; right now I decide to go and find a café outside to have a beer and then get a taxi back to my pension in Lavacolla. I figure if I wander a bit through the old town I'll find what I need and so it is. I look up and see that I've entered the 'Plaza Cervantes' and there's a statue of the scribe to prove it, complete with his little beard and rakish moustache, and I could tilt at a windmill in joy as I order a beer in a lovely little bar. My phone beeps and it's a text from Hannah. She is staying in Santiago until Friday and asks if I would like to meet up with her, which of course I'm delighted to do and that's my last night sorted. Her text reminds me to deposit the postcard she gave me in a box so I spend another half hour finding a stamp and postbox.

At dinner that night I see Marcia, Tom and the gang who are just finishing up their meal so I have a quick chat before I'm seated. They tell me that when they were in their hotel in Palais del Rei they were sitting at an outside bar next to a group of Italian cyclists who seemed to be getting quite excited about something and when they looked they saw it was me striding by at my usual lick. Who knew?! Marcia thinks I should move to Italy. I'm so happy to be going to mass tomorrow and to be wearing a dress; Marcia talks of little else. They tell me they are looking forward to not having to do washing every night.

I'm exhausted, and after a lovely dinner and half a bottle of the chilled local red wine I turn in. As I switch off the light it hits me, I've done it! I've completed my walk and I don't have to walk tomorrow. I can't quite get my head round it.

CHAPTER 14

MAY THE CAMINO
RISE UP TO MEET YOU

It is an absolute joy to shower, wash my hair and put on clean jeans (a little looser than they were over a week ago, I might add, despite the carbs) and a pair of comfy loafers. I fold up my sticks and eye my packed suitcase suspiciously. I'm determined that when I go to check in tomorrow I will not pay a penny excess baggage. I'll look at what I can get rid of and how I can make it lighter when I'm at the hotel in Santiago tonight. But now I want breakfast. A group of walkers, who are not English but I can't make out where they are from, are already halfway through theirs and seem to be irritating the waiter serving them. They are still on their first coffee but are asking for another, and the waiter tells them something to the effect that they only have one coffee included with their breakfast before turning his back abruptly on them. They eventually leave and he comes over to me. I'm a little daunted as he was quite stern with the other group but he turns a brilliant smile on me and I try in Spanish to tell him I want to leave with the luggage if that would be possible. His English is quite good and he says he will phone my travel company and see what time the luggage is being picked up. I finish my coffee and croissant as he returns to say that he will get the travel company on the phone but first, would I like another coffee? I would indeed.

After breakfast the owner of the hotel, a lovely older lady who speaks no English, takes me into her office to call the travel company. They tell me that it will be fine to go with the luggage van but that it won't be there until between 10am and 10.30am. I figure it would be daft to pay fifteen euros for a taxi and although it's only 8.15am I'll wait. I scribble these times down on a pad and the owner, who is standing by me, indicates excitedly that she wants to talk to the travel company so I pass her the phone; she speaks in rapid Spanish for a minute or so then passes the phone back to me. It transpires that she is going to Santiago in half an hour and would like to drive me there herself. I am so touched by this I give her a huge hug and as I pull away see that we both have tears in our eyes and both start to laugh at being so slushy so early in the day. My luggage will still go by van later on but I won't have to sit around.

Today I feel charmed. As I'm dropped in the middle of town I wonder how I'll find my hotel but I'm not too worried, it's a beautiful day and still early so I wander down a cobbled street and as I turn the corner come face to face with my hotel. I hadn't even got the guidebook out but had remembered the name. It is very small and covered in ivy. Inside it's very chic and minimalist. The receptionist is lovely and reminds me of the gorgeous one in Leon. I'm so happy I won't be traumatising her. I've been told that the mass will be very busy and that I should aim to get there at 11am for the noon kick-off. I tell the receptionist I need to get something from my luggage when it arrives and she says it might not be there until as late as 11.30am. I have to wear my dress, Marcia expects it! The receptionist takes down my mobile number and says she'll let me know when it arrives. Given today's vibe, I just know it will arrive in time.

She directs me off to explore in the old town and in particular a wonderful old building that houses the market. Now I'm in a city it seems so crowded to me. It's a shock to the system as I've been used to small villages. I also realise that being in a city makes me miss Jimmy, this having been his natural habitat. Our plan had been that after Christmas we would organise renting out our house and then take a small flat in the centre of London, somewhere around his beloved Drury Lane. We'd even toyed with renting for a short time in another of our favourite cities, Paris. Why not? We had the flexibility of work and would be able to afford it through the rental income from our house. We were both so excited at the prospect and it was yet another dream snuffed out by his death. Another sliding-doors scenario. I'm feeling a bit weepy as I drink my coffee opposite the market but just then a text comes in to my phone to say my luggage has arrived and I'm instantly cheered. It's 10.40am and I'm back in the hotel, changed into the dress and at the cathedral just after 11am.

Already the pews in the cathedral are almost full. But my charmed day continues as I spot Marcia halfway down the cathedral with the family and they've nabbed a pew. She jumps up and hugs me and yells 'God bless you!' and I know she means it. She then asks how I knew where they would be and I explain it's just one of those days. The six of us cram onto the pew and the show begins. About five priests are on the 'stage' and a nun. I quietly name her Maria. And it turns out to be quite apt as she begins by teaching us how to sing parts of the service; 'let's start at the very beginning' comes to mind. The Fulhams know the drill, though, without any lessons. This is their religion but it does feel like we are all more than welcome. The altar is incredibly ornate and I sit back and let the service wash over me and get up and down when prompted and mumble along by way of participating. I'm at the end of the pew and get a blessing from a priest and then the drama peaks when what appears to be an enormous, silver wrecking ball swings across in front of the priests spouting vast amounts of incense. I gather that it's only lit on special occasions and today happens to be a Feast Day – ah, that Camino, I love it. The Catholics really do put on a show. Eleanor tells me that I was mentioned as a pilgrim from London walking from Leon; I've somehow missed it in the excitement but I'm over the moon to hear that I got a name check. There are a group of Germans recording the mass who are told to stop, but then I spy a couple of priests taking pictures. Then it comes to the communion part. Because of the sheer volume of folk crammed into the cathedral it would take half a day to get through everyone so instead wafers are passed round on silver salvers a little like a catered party. No wine but it seems to do the job for those participating. I politely refuse the wafers and am content with my earlier blessing.

As we part company outside the cathedral I get my photo taken with the Fulham family and we swap addresses and hugs. They've been such a treat on my trip. I'm absolutely starving and have a hankering for a *bocadillo*, but a good one, and instinctively let the road lead me, and it does. I happen across a place that appears to be full of locals called Café Belke and I have the absolutely most delicious artisan bread filled with ham and cheese. There's not a single *peregrino* shell, walking stick or piece of bad footwear in sight.

The only indicator that I'm part of the walking crowd is my backpack.

I go back to my hotel and embark on the re-packing, I am so determined not to get shafted by that bloody airline. I start by getting rid of any unnecessary weighty items so decide to leave behind my shampoo and conditioner, and the only other thing that is bulky is the book, which I've finished so leave it in the room too. I then figure I can wear my heavy walking boots on the plane and put as much as I can in my backpack for hand luggage as this doesn't get weighed. I've no idea if I've done a good enough job when I'm finished but am too tired to really care and opt for a wee siesta. The room is really lovely and I feel so special having completed the last part of the journey and experiencing the mass at the cathedral. Sleep comes very easily.

I sleep for much longer than I intended and it's late afternoon when I wake and see I've a text from Hannah saying that they are in town and would I like to meet for a farewell drink tonight? I certainly would. The bar isn't very far from my hotel and I stroll round in the warm evening air to find a group of very young, very handsome people gathered in an outrageously trendy hostelry. And in the middle is lovely Hannah looking radiant. She leaps up from her group when she sees me and I hear a delightful young man say 'So, is this Saint Claire?' Apparently my good deed/sleepover has gone down as a mitzvah and I've been canonised by them. It's a wonderful feeling although quite undeserved as I had such fun when they stayed. I hang out for a couple of drinks but then leave them to their youth. They plan to head to the coastal town of Finisterre tomorrow, which will mean they've gone as far west as they can on the Camino. The 'end of the earth', quite literally, for them.

CHAPTER 15

HOMECOMING

As I take my luggage down to reception it hits me that today it's actually coming with me. A taxi has been booked and I'm surprised by the massive black Mercedes that arrives to whisk me away from the Camino to the airport. We drive past Lavacolla and I spot a couple of walkers navigating the last leg of their Camino looking exhausted as I sink back into the air-conditioned comfort of the plush leather seats and ponder my next, most important challenge. No, not going back to south-east London and navigating my life post this experience; I'm thinking about getting my luggage onto that plane without paying a penny. They will not mug me for 50 euros this time around.

I stand in line at the check-in feeling odd wearing my walking boots and with my backpack weighing a ton. I watch the Spanish couple in front of me being sent off to pay their fine and as I step up to the desk I all but crack my knuckles before placing my suitcase on the scales. The pause is interminable as the numbers go up and down and I almost expect to hear a drum roll. But the woman at the desk just lifts her head and it's over as she places the white label through the handle and presses the ends together before pushing the button to send it on its way to the hold and handing me back my passport and boarding card. I feel like shouting 'yes' and doing a lap of honour but instead I treat myself to a final *café con leche*.

It's really a peculiar feeling to be leaving the life of the Camino. The security of getting up, having breakfast prepared and knowing that the day will feature nothing more than walking, walking, walking. Then eating, writing and sleeping to awake to more of the same. It's a very comforting way to live and I'm incredibly reluctant to leave it.

As I stand at the luggage carousel at Stansted Airport the Camino sprinkles one last piece of magic when I see my suitcase is the first out, the very first. That's never happened to me before in my life! As I wheel it off to the Stansted Express with no arrows to follow, no backpacked walkers to overtake, I feel ok. I don't need arrows. I can find my own way now with the road rising up to meet me. Standing in the queue waiting to buy my train ticket I chat to a woman who sees my walking boots and asks about the Camino. We chat for a while and I'm about to tell her I'm a widow but you know what? I decide not to. I'm going home.

THE END

EPILOGUE

SEVEN YEARS LATER

Apparently, it takes seven years for every cell in our bodies to regenerate. This means that just seven years after any given event you are, on a cellular level at least, a completely different person – like a broom that's had both its handle and its brush replaced. Of course if you get down to the nitty gritty things are a little more complicated than that, but personally I like the idea a lot and will take it for myself. It is, in fact, seven years since I walked the Camino and such a lot has happened since then that I can say, hand on heart, that my entire being has changed. Really nothing is the same. I moved house. I had to; it was too big and I couldn't afford the mortgage on my own. I bought a flat with my older brother and found out that we get on surprisingly well. My two cats shuffled off this mortal coil and in their place I now have four cats (which along with widowhood, puts me firmly in 'mad cat lady' territory – I don't mind). I never replaced Jimmy. What's the expression – 'women grieve and men replace'?

Harsh perhaps but regardless, no one could match up to him so it just seemed futile to look. In some strange way, having had the love-of-my-life, albeit for such a relatively brief time, I know that part of me will never be taken and the knowledge of his love is enough to sustain me.

One thing I am immensely proud of is that the drama we had been working on before he died, *Nightshift*, was eventually filmed. I produced it for Sky TV and they even put 'In memory of Jimmy Gardner' at the end of it. He would have been so chuffed. His words got to reach an audience even after his death.

Jimmy had a friend who had planted three Scots pines at the top of a hill in a lovely big park in south-east London: one for his wife and one for each of his sons. We had always loved this idea and after Jimmy died the same friend offered to get one planted for him. A year after his death we had a tribute night for Jimmy with friends and family, speeches and a screening of one of Jimmy's earlier TV shows. The next day we went to the park and planted the tree, including some of his ashes next to the roots. The tree thrives today sitting in what we call *Scots Corner* with the other three trees and at Christmas I put tartan ribbons on the branches and take the pine cones to decorate with glitter for my own Christmas tree. I love the idea of Jimmy's ashes being a part of the tree and it's a lovely place to go to all year round.

Unfortunately, I can't share any enlightening words of wisdom about how grief will affect you (and it will affect you in some form) or the best way to deal with it. All I can say is that it does get easier, it just has to. It's cliché, but the truth is that you can't have an ending without a beginning. My life changed for the better once I was able to turn to face forward again and weave dreams to follow once more. I had lost my dreaming partner but miraculously found I still had the capacity to dream. Once I realised this, I knew that I would be ok, that I would never stop missing and loving Jimmy but that the burden of grief I'd been carrying had transformed into a protective cloak made from Jimmy's love that I could wear no matter what life had planned for me.

Jimmy wrote beautiful poetry and we both used to adore reading poems aloud to one another. He did a great rendition of *Howl* and I think Allen Ginsberg would have loved to hear it read in Jimmy's broad Scots accent. I think Somerset Maugham got it right when he said 'The crown of literature is poetry. It is its end and aim. It is the sublimest activity of the human mind. It is the achievement of beauty. The writer of prose can only step aside when the poet passes; he makes the best of us look like a piece of cheese.'

With that in mind, I've decided to share a couple of Jimmy's poems.

*He wrote this one after the last miscarriage, and we quoted the
final two lines in the order of service at his funeral as they seemed
to sum up Jimmy's attitude to life so perfectly.*

She Carries the Banner for Life

In a glimpse of a moment,
Life with all its joy, its pain,
Encoded in a smidgin,
A haricot bean,
Alive in a universe unseen.
Hopping over puddles,
Widen-eyes at animal shadows,
And later – a shard of me and you,
Rolled into a body and heart and soul
Pushing a plate away,
Wearing wellies in the snow.
And all the hope and disappointment,
Lives only in the love,
A joy unfurled,
A day unannounced,
An unblinking universe.
In pain and a cold brisk side ward,
All the product of our love.
In a lake spilt by fate
It feels like a love unrequited,

A letter unopened.

A day that never dawns,

Light dances across a wet branch,

And looks like maybe a Sprite…!

But as we turn to wonder

Vanishes – trick of the eye,

We wonder if we saw it at all.

But the love that fights for the human heart,

Stares into the maw of the unblinking universe,

Dares forever its endless sorrows.

Braver than regiments,

Refuses ever to bow to the Hate.

All life, however fleeting, spits its triumph

Into the cold eye of Death.

And this one he wrote after our wedding day:

My Heart

One year ago I stood, heart banging among the purple flowers,
Among kilts and gilded mirrors and gearing up for flight,
And lost and all alone and reckoning the distance to the door,
Then saw at last your face appear and knew it all alright.

I screwed up my eyes to see you and could only take your hand
And talk to your fingers, felt yours gently press on mine.
I supposed you looked beautiful as when were you anything less.
Could not see but only glimpse sidelong your lovely eye and grin.

As I slipped that ring on your finger all ceased and turned.
Calm fell over me like that of ages, of rivers and of mountains.
I felt all the dead still centre not just of the room but my life whole
Time ceased and I will hear the moment forever. I will hear
the moment forever and the moment is you my love.

Lightning Source UK Ltd.
Milton Keynes UK
UKHW012311240819
348542UK00001B/32/P